Contents

Preface

The story goes that a successful businessman wanted to have a family tree prepared by a genealogist. The latter, finding that the tycoon's great-grandfather had died in the electric chair in Sing-Sing after committing a horrible murder, wired: 'Find discreditable ancestors. Do you wish me to continue search?' The laconic reply came: 'Proceed.' Months later the businessman received a copy of his family tree and was surprised and delighted to read the entry beside the name of his great-grandfather. It went thus: 'Occupied the Chair of Applied Electricity in a distinguished New York institution. Died in harness.' This story's moral is that it is easy to improve one's ancestry if only one's origins are humble. It may be a consolation for some of the more recent religious movements, especially when it is recalled that St Paul said of the earliest Christians, 'Not many wise, not many noble are called.' In any case, I have tried to tell the story of all the religious movements without snobbery or superiority, remembering that Adam is our common ancestor and that the New Adam, Christ, rehabilitates us all.

The two most recent religious movements are the Jesus Freaks (only five years of age) and Scientology (less than thirty). Each of them has a brand new chapter devoted to it in this third revised edition of *Christian Deviations*.

In addition, four chapters have been completely rewritten in the light of further research and with the benefit of monographs written since the appearance of the last edition. In some cases I have been able to improve these chapters with the help of courteous and informed criticism of representatives of the movements described. In other cases, friends of mine have provided fuller information which I have been glad to use.

Mr Gilbert U. H. Murray of Willowdale, Ontario, Canada, sent me a long critical letter on the movement to which he belongs, the Seventh-Day Adventists. The rewritten chapter on the Mormons owes much to two members of the Church of Jesus Christ of Latter-Day Saints, Mr Gordon E. Banks of Albuquerque, New Mexico, and Professor Milton V. Backman, Jr, of Brigham Young University. The former sent me a carefully documented letter of twenty-four pages and the latter provided a rectifying review in *Dialogue: a Journal of Mormon Thought* (Volume 1, Number 2, Summer 1966). My revised chapter on the Spiritualists makes a distinction between Christian Spiritualists and all other Spiritualists. This clarification I owe to a letter sent by Mr Leslie Price written when he was an undergraduate majoring in Religious Studies in the University of Sussex. My chapter on Christian Science has been greatly improved by the constructive criticisms and careful documentation of my friend, the Reverend David McIlhiney of Princeton University. To all my correspondents I express my deep sense of gratitude.

The perceptive reader will note that some of the religious movements I treat in these pages are relatively close to historic Christianity (such are the Jesus Freaks and the Seventh-Day Adventists). He will also observe that yet others add to Christian sources other scriptures than the Old and New Testaments (such are Christian Science and the Mormons). Both these groups and those like them warrant the classification 'Christian *Deviations*'. A third group, of which Theosophy and Scientology are the sole members to be treated in this book, are alternatives to, rather than deviations from, Christianity. They are, however, significant religious movements deserving of study in their own right.

Again I express the sincere hope that this book will facilitate fair dialogue and discussion between representatives of the historic Christian churches associated with the World Council of Churches and members of the new religious movements. For this to be successful there must be open-mindedness and charity on both sides of the present divide. Certainly this is too serious a time for the perpetuation of bias or bigotry. Dialogue presupposes accuracy and honesty.

H.D.

1 The Sociology of Sectarianism

*Be ready always to answer every man
that asketh you a reason of the hope
that is in you ...* (I Peter 3.15)

It is a paradox that the present century, which has witnessed the greatest growth of the ecumenical movement for the reunion of the divided Christian churches, has also seen the fastest expansion of the sects and cults which split Christendom further apart. The 'great new fact of our time' (as Archbishop William Temple termed the ecumenical movement) is counterbalanced by the great *old* fact of our time – the renewal of heresy and schism.

So strong are some of these new movements that they can no longer be regarded as harmless oddities and eccentric deviations from the historic norms of Christian faith, worship and behaviour. Their very success in perpetuating error, strife and bitterness constitutes their challenge and menace to the historic Christian churches.

Our concern in the present chapter is threefold. It is, in the first place, to recognize fully that the most Christian of these deviations have demonstrated a remarkable growth in numbers, in the expansion of their missionary activities and in the most modern means of propaganda, in recent decades. Secondly, we shall consider the confusion caused by sectarian Christianity on the mission-field and its betrayal of Christ's will for unity among his disciples. Thirdly, an attempt will be made to account for the dynamic appeal of the sects, not in terms of their doctrinal deviations, for this will be the concern of Chapter 12, but from the standpoint of their social cohesiveness, their simple authoritarianism, their emotional warmth and similar factors.

I

All the available statistics (and they are difficult to find) show that the sects are experiencing an increase in membership of between three and nine per cent per annum. It will be well to begin with the missionary Mormons, or, to give them their official title, the Church of Jesus Christ of Latter-Day Saints. As if to mark the gauntlet which this American cult has thrown down to the stable and religiously conservative British people, the Mormons have recently built a vast modern temple in the metropolis, across the road from London's intellectual hub and mind, the South Kensington Science Museum. This new building, with its gold-leaved spirelet, is a powerful symbol of aggressive sectarianism. In 1962 there were ninety-three churches and an estimated community of over 11,000.[1] The Mormon leaders told one observer that fifty new churches were planned in Britain in three years.[2]

The success of Mormonism is almost entirely due to its marvellous missionary organization. World membership in this religious community now numbers about 3,500,000. It has over 10,000 missionaries in the field and it expects to gain many more missionaries in the near future. Fifty per cent of the members in good standing and in good health are expected to venture on a two-year missionary journey, often at their own expense for travel and maintenance, to whatever part of the world they may be sent from the headquarters at Salt Lake City, Utah. He or she may go to South Africa, to Switzerland, or even New Zealand. This is, indeed, a most vigorous expression of the Protestant principle of the priesthood of all believers. Often these missionaries are in the very prime of health and strength and their candid, outgoing personalities make a great impression through their zeal and radiant integrity of life. Is it, then, surprising that these young ambassadors are partly responsible for a three per cent per annum increase in Mormon membership?

The rate of growth of the Seventh-Day Adventists is even more striking. In 1950 membership of the movement was given as 225,000. In 1960 it was 305,000. In 1971 they numbered over 400,000, an annual increase of about nine per cent.[3]

The statistics of the Spiritualists in the United States also show a remarkable increase. Between 1950 and 1960 estimated membership grew from 126,000 to 175,000, a rate of forty-four per cent.[4] However, the very nature of the movement makes accurate figures hard to come by.

The most active proselytizers among the sects are the Jehovah's Witnesses, who believe that all governments and all the Christian churches are in abysmal error. By means of a mammoth publishing programme, radio propaganda, and an army of tract-sellers with the pertinacity of successful commercial travellers who make frequent 'back-calls', they are the best-known, if not the best-liked, of all the sects in the English-speaking world. They well deserve the appellation of aggressive missionaries. It is known for certain that in the decade from 1942 to 1952 their numbers doubled in North America, multiplied fifteen times in South America, twelve times in the Atlantic islands, five times in Asia, seven times in Europe and Africa, and six times in the Pacific islands. In 1966, they claimed to have 1,109,806 members in about 200 countries. Their leading publication, *The Watchtower*, has grown from an initial circulation of 6,000 copies in 1879 to over three million copies per month in 1960. It is no less significant that *The Watchtower* is published in forty-six different languages.[5]

It should already be clear that the remarkable recent growth of these and other sects and the dissemination of their views by enthusiastic missionaries and through the medium of the radio and the printed page, constitute a serious challenge to the Christian church. If their work were only among the pagans or the uncommitted of the modern world, then concern for their success might rightly be interpreted as a dog-in-the-manger attitude. The great danger, however, comes from the arrogant dogmatism with which most of them claim that they alone have the full and untainted truth and from their often successful attempts to steal sheep from other folds of the Christian church.

Moreover, for anyone who takes seriously to heart the high-priestly prayer of Jesus that 'they may all be one', the sight of ever-increasing fragmentation of Christendom is intolerable. Jesus, as recorded by the Fourth Evangelist, evidently wished his beloved community, the church, to manifest the divine love on earth which characterized his own relationship with the Father, 'so that the world may believe'. The root objection to sectarianism is that it provides for a world already split into suspicious political, racial and social camps, not the secret of a supernatural unity, but the competition of the arrogant and the vindictive. Thus, the life and death of Jesus, which had as its aim reconciliation and atonement, is betrayed by a Christendom not at one, but at odds. Therefore, indeed, the world will not believe. The denominations have been at fault, and the new movements have splintered the witness even further.

II

The bewilderment and confusion caused by competitive sects is strikingly illustrated from both the sending and the receiving countries on the mission-field.

Bishop Azariah of India once pleaded at an ecumenical conference that the European churches should cease to introduce into India sixteenth- and seventeenth-century differences of Protestant doctrinal emphasis (Calvinist or Arminian) and of church government (Episcopalian, Presbyterian and Congregational), as they were increasingly irrelevant in Europe and wholly irrelevant in India. He made the further point that there was no justification in calling out Hindus from a religious caste-system, only to place them in a Christian denominational caste-system. The point, with reference to the vast land of China was wittily put by the missionary who asked : What have the Southern Baptists to do with the North Chinese?

A personal experience of mine while I was living in the Republic of South Africa, may be apposite here. I found that three different groups of African Congregationalists were under the impression that they belonged to three separate denominations. One group described themselves as 'CUSA' Christians; another group called themselves 'LMS' Christians; while a third group wished to be known as 'ABCFM' Christians. The interpretation of this rash of initials meant that the first group had been evangelized by the Congregational Union of South Africa, an indigenous South African expression of Congregationalism. The second group were the converts of the British London Missionary Society. The third group were the members of the flock of the American Board of Commissioners for Foreign Missions, with headquarters in Boston, Massachusetts. Confusion could hardly be more complete! The groups have since united, but what makes so untimely the chaos of the sects is that the newly emerging Africa, with its several autonomous republics, has so often confused essential Christianity with its European trappings and American overclothes, not to mention the association with a white racial superiority (less often expressed by missionaries than by other settlers, let it be said!), that they may be tempted to reject Christianity altogether as incompatible with a virile independency.

In the South African Republic the government officially recognizes over a thousand different sects! Thus African tribalism has repaid the confusion with which competing denominations and competitive sects have disseminated their tenets. It is extraordinarily difficult for the most perceptive African (and European, for that matter) to disentangle essential Christianity from the cultural envelopes in which it is enclosed, when he is offered the Christian faith and worship by Polish Roman Catholics, Swedish Lutherans, Anglican High Churchmen, American Congregationalists, British Methodists, Afrikaners of the Apostolic Church Mission, and from Presbyterians who are British, Dutch and French, to take but a few notable examples from South Africa. How much greater, then, is the confusion caused to those taking their first halting steps in the Christian way when the sects make confusion worse confounded! It is not merely embarrassing or inconvenient, it is a scandal – a tearing of the seamless robe of Christ at a time when the historic Christian churches are deeply penitent for their 'unhappy divisions'.

It is, perhaps, of unusual interest that most of the groups which will be considered in the following pages first took their rise in the United States of America. This is true of Christian Science, with its headquarters in Boston, Massachusetts; of the largest Pentecostal body, the Assemblies of God, with headquarters at Springfield, Missouri; of the Seventh-Day Adventists, with headquarters in Washington, DC; of the Mormons, with headquarters in Salt Lake City, Utah; of the Jehovah's Witnesses, with headquarters in Brooklyn, New York State; of the National Spiritualist Association, with headquarters in Milwaukee, Wisconsin; and it is also true of Moral Re-Armament which was founded by an American Lutheran, Frank Buchman, and of Scientology, founded by Ron Hubbard.

The fact that so many groups originated in the United States is occasionally attributed by the unthinking to the inherent viciousness of the American temperament, and often by persons who accuse Americans in the same breath of a deplorable tendency to social conformity. The deeper reasons for the vigorous variety of denominations and sects in the United States are two. In the first place, when the United States first came into being as an independent nation (no longer an overseas colony of Britain), the founding fathers determined that there should be a complete separation of church and state. No single established church could have met the needs of the new nation, with Congregationalism predominant in New England, Presbyterianism in the Mid-Atlantic States, Anglicanism in Virginia and New York State, Quakerism in Pennsylvania, Roman Catholicism in Maryland, and significant groups of Lutherans, Methodists and Baptists elsewhere. In consequence no denomination was favoured, and so each had to set to vigorously about the task of raising its finances to pay its minister and to erect buildings suitable for worship and Christian education. An aggressive missionary spirit is therefore characteristic of American Protestantism and Catholicism, as is a plurality of denominations and groups accorded equal status before the law.

The second factor accounting for the spread of new cults was the remarkable extension of the westward-moving frontier in the nineteenth century. Here the rugged individuals who pioneered the new trails through the mid-West to the coast of California would not be content with the traditional and staid church ways of the Eastern seaboard. They desired and obtained a more spontaneous expression of religion, such as the camp-meeting revivalists provided, a faith in which they co-operated with God for their salvation, and a form of church government in which they managed their own church affairs without dictation from hierarchy or connexion. New prophets, like Joseph Smith the Mormon leader, or William Miller, the Adventist founder, found in the optimistic and millennial atmosphere a ready hearing for an indigenously American revelation or new interpretations of the old faith.

If, however, Americans planted the largest crop of new groups, it should not be forgotten that they have also been deeply concerned for the reintegration of a split Christendom. It should be recalled that the famous Lambeth Quadrilateral of 1920, which formulated the basis on which the Anglican bridge-church was prepared to welcome unity with other Protestant communions without sacrificing its Catholic heritage of the ecumenical creeds and the threefold and historic ministry, was only reiterating proposals that American Episcopalians had formulated in Chicago several decades before. Huntingdon, Bishop Brent and John R. Mott are as important names in the ecumenical roll of fame as are Archbishop William Temple, Bishop George Bell, and Archbishop Nathan Söderblom on the other side of the Atlantic. Furthermore, in the study of the non-theological factors that have promoted separation among the churches, Professor H. Richard Niebuhr's *The Social Sources of Denominationalism* is as penetrating a study of the modern period as Professor S. L. Greenslade's *Schism in the Early Church* is of the period of the church fathers. Moreover, there have been important mergers of separate churches in the United States to give proof that there is a strong will to ecumenism in that vast country.

The growth of the new groups has been described as 'the unpaid bill of the churches'. This epigram may be interpreted as meaning that these groups exist to stress those doctrinal elements or practices which the historic churches have neglected or ignored. That this is a centrally important factor in accounting for the rise of the new groups will be argued in Chapter 12 of this book. The epigram is also true in another sense: that is, that various non-doctrinal factors of a social and cultural nature are also responsible for the rise of the groups. It is to an examination of these sociological factors that we now turn.

It is undeniable that many groups, and even denominations, come into being simply because the existing churches or denominations have lost their early fervour and become strongholds of the respectable and circumspect middle classes. These new groups or denominations, therefore, show all the characteristics of 'churches of the disinherited' (as H. Richard Niebuhr terms them). They are consciously established as the refuges of the poor. The Baptists, the Quakers and the Methodists began in this way. As their members rose in the economic scale, became more cultured and began to compromise their original world-renouncing ethics, those left behind in the social struggle drew apart into separate and congenial groupings. It is such folk who constitute the main support of the contemporary cults, such as the Pentecostalists, the Seventh-Day Adventists and the Jehovah's Witnesses, although prosperity is improving the social status of the first two groups. Royston Pike says of the Jehovah's Witnesses that:

> The heaven that is preached in Kingdom Hall is the sort of place that may well appeal to the man who knows what unemployment means, who has had to tighten his belt, who works at a monotonous job, who has tried to bring up his family in a smelly little box of a place. It is the sort of place that will appeal to the woman who has had to share a kitchen and has had too many children when she didn't want them, and had to nurse a girl with polio or mourn a baby that hardly lived to breathe.[6]

This is the religion of the hard-pressed and frustrated, who, without such faith and the company of their fellows at the bottom of the social scale, would be the utterly defeated. Suspicious of an educated ministry, or formal ritual and ceremonial, they find the greatest satisfaction in the emotional freedom, the naïve supernaturalism, the vivid personal sermons with crude rhetorical devices and the democratic forms of church government, which the parent denominations have outgrown. It is also significant that they exalt the simple manners, necessitated by their indigence, into moral virtues.[7] Honesty, thrift, abstinence, simplicity, diligence – these reflect their economic position almost as much as their moral ideals.

It is also significant that it is among such groups that millennial ideas have spread. These are, indeed, the defence-mechanisms of the disinherited. The reward for poverty in time is an eternity spent walking on golden streets. Despairing of obtaining substantial advantages from the usual and all-too-gradual social processes, they reject the world that first rejected them, and they eagerly await the cosmic cataclysm that will cast down the mighty from their seats and exalt the humble and meek. In consequence, the leaders of the sects laud the God who is 'the help of the helpless', while the leaders of the longer established churches seem to serve a God who 'helps those who help themselves'. The ultimate vindication of the 'saints' is, for the sects, the thousand years of the rule of Christ preceded by Armageddon; for the members of the *bourgeois* and comfortable denominations the vindication of religious faith is the establishment of religion as a way of life that will promote greater brotherhood among men and the elimination of social tensions. As the sectarians look beyond time for entry into the kingdom of heaven, so do the historic denominations await a kingdom of God upon earth. As their eschatological ideas differ, so do their conceptions of God. For the sects God is conceived in transcendent, irruptionist manner, 'terrible as an army with banners', the God of hosts, terrible in wrath to the worldlings, but inexpressibly gracious to his elect. For the denominations, God is conceived as an indwelling Deity, whose will is gradually fulfilled in the processes of nature and society, at the promptings of benevolence.

Sectarianism has its own distinctive code of ethics, as we have hinted already, and this is a corollary of its worldly estate. It is a legalistic, rigid, Puritan, black-and-white morality which divides men and women all too easily into world-affirming goats and world-renouncing sheep, or, in other words, into children of darkness and children of light. The vices are merely the practices of the opulent. Hence the sectarians ban such worldly amusements as dancing, cinema and theatregoing, the use of tobacco and of alcoholic drinks. They despise all ostentation and all literature, art and music that is not propaganda, for their particular tenets, as wholly mundane. On the positive side, austerity of life, self-denial in things naturally desired, abstinence and mortification of the flesh, are the moral foundations of their code. There is, indeed, an attractive, if spurious, simplicity and exhilaration in the world-renouncing ethics of the sectarians, and it provides their communities with a firm cohesion and unity. Nonetheless, it is a naïve simplicity, for the world cannot be divided so conveniently into sinners and saints, since both cohabit in the same person. Moreover, sectarianism has its own subtle temptations to pride and uncharitableness. For this reason a transformist ethic, for all its agonies of decision made in the twilight of imperfect choices and inevitable compromises, seems preferable to a fugitive ethics of renunciation.

If the *bourgeois* complacency of many of the existing denominations has made the members of the sects feel unwelcome, they also make them feel emotionally starved. For members of the historic denominations, whose education makes them more emotionally restrained, rare attempts are made by the festivals of the Christian year, 'Dedication Sundays' or such devices, to renew a sense of the great convictions that transform men from the top of the mind to the bottom of the heart. On the whole, however, the comfortable find emotional outlets in cultural associations and social recreations usually outside the churches. For the sectarians, however, religious community provides the whole of their life. Indeed, the sectarians deliberately adopt devices to stir up the emotions and, with complete sincerity, they attribute the results to the direct activity of God, the Holy Spirit.

The perfectionist sects, in particular, seem to insist that an emotional reaction is the only *proof* that the individual soul has made direct contact with God. Christianity for them becomes a religion of feeling. For this reason they particularly covet 'blessings' – gifts and outpourings of the Holy Spirit, *charismata*. In an ascending series they long for the experiences, first, of conversion and forgiveness, next of holiness or the 'second blessing', which gives an inner sense of complete purgation and harmony with the will of God, and, thirdly, the gift of tongues, visions, prophecies, which correspond to the mystical state of 'spiritual marriage'. In consequence, they prefer a simpler, spontaneous, highly-charged emotional service to the use of any liturgy. Their hymns are sung to urgent, staccato rhythms and tunes that are as easily memorized as the simple words, with their repeated choruses. The prayers are highly personal and extemporary, and they are often punctuated by fervent cries of 'Hallelujah' and 'Amen'. The preaching is also extemporary and frequently crudely rhetorical in character, with passionate denunciations of the worldly, tender appeals to accept Christ as Saviour, horrific accounts of hell or the more-likely-to-be-realized eschatology of the atomic bomb, and simple testimonies to the protecting power of God. The appeal is rarely to the reason, almost always to the emotions.

Another characteristic of the sects is their craving for objectivity and authority. The members seem to demand of their leaders that they give them certainties, since they have enough doubts of their own. As they find the black-and-white ethical code a respite from the responsibility of weighing motives, intentions and results, so they cannot bear the burden of thinking out the Christian faith anew in the light of modern thought. They are conservative biblical literalists in most articles of belief and they appear to believe that all persons must think alike. Utterly suspicious of tradition, they would eliminate all the centuries of Christian thought and experience between the first and the present as a prolonged era of apostasy. They believe it to be their duty to reproduce the primitive church in all its fullness as described in the pages of the New Testament. This attitude follows inevitably from their belief that the Bible is the infallibly inspired Word of God and that it contains the Christian faith, including all details of organization and administration which have been 'once for all delivered to the saints'. Allied to this conviction that they constitute the only true church of Christ, however small their numbers, is the bitter necessity to condemn all other Christians.

We have already indicated how class distinction within the historic Christian churches, allied to a *bourgeois* complacency, has frozen out the perfervid sectarians. An equally important factor in promoting divisiveness and sectarianism has been racial exclusiveness, especially in countries where there are ethnic minorities. Professor Bengt Sundkler has shown in fascinating detail in his *Bantu Prophets in South Africa* how the indigenous African cults, as offshoots of Christianity, have arisen as protests against the arrogance of the white man. Sometimes they have taken the form of mating African nationalism with Christianity; at other times they manifest an extreme other-worldliness in which eternity is the compensation for a lowly status in time; at yet other times they include much African tribal lore and corybantic customs which the staid faith of the missionaries condemns.[8] Similarly, Professor H. Richard Niebuhr shows in *The Social Sources of Denominationalism* that Negro cults and denominations come into being to protest against their members being accommodated in separate parts of the white church where their supposed superiors seem to worship a white tribal Deity, or in order to have their more charismatic and emotional type of worship and to perform the duties and responsibilities of governing themselves in states where they were not allowed to exercise any civic responsibilities.

Perhaps the most pathetic example of the failure of the dominant white Christians in fellowship being responsible for the establishment of a Negro cult is to be found in the Afro-American church named 'The Church of the Living God, Christian Workers for Fellowship'. Its leader, Mrs Ethel Christian, claimed that she could prove from scripture that Jesus was a Negro.[9] Arguing that Christ was the Son of David, and David the author of the Psalms, she claimed that the 119th Psalm proved her point. For there the Psalmist declares, 'I am become like a bottle in the smoke'. It is more relevant to lament the prejudice of the white Christians than to deplore the oddities of Afro-American exegesis.

IV

If the analysis of the part played by sociological factors in the acceleration of sectarianism is at all valid, then its meaning for the historic Christian churches is readily seen. It is surely most important to recognize that the historic Christian churches have been in considerable part responsible for the various revulsions that brought the sects into being. It is equally important to recognize that not all the blame can be laid at the feet of the denominations, for often the leaders of sectarian groups have been excluded by religious discipline from the historic churches; sometimes they have been men of greater personal ambition and greed for power than men of spiritual vision. But the charge has sufficient relevance to make it imperative for the Christian church to become in reality what it is in principle, the inclusive and beloved community. Dante saw inscribed over the portals of hell the words, 'Abandon hope, all ye who enter here.' The Christian should see in his mind's eye, as he enters the portal of every Christian church, the legend, 'Abandon all distinctions, ye who enter here.' Then the church of Christ would be in fact what St Paul maintained it was in principle, one where 'there shall be neither Jew nor Greek, neither bond nor free, neither male nor female, but all one man in Christ Jesus'. A church which perpetuates, instead of transcending, worldly divisions is already guilty of segregating and therefore of its own type of sectarianism, and is, of course, a great instigator of sectarianism.

If the churches by their racial or class prejudices have become enclaves of arrogance or complacency, then they must bear the blame for the alienation of the under-privileged which resulted in the formation of sects as communities for the poor and disinherited. The cure for arrogance is that humility which comes from the common recognition that all men stand in need of forgiveness, and the condition for receiving God's forgiveness is that we exercise it towards others. The cure for race prejudice and class exclusiveness is both a Christian colour and class blindness and active dedication to the pursuit of social justice.

Again, if the historic churches have diluted their doctrine with the waters of modernistic compromise, or, to vary the metaphor, if they have muffled the strong trumpet of revelation, which condemns before it consoles, so that it gives forth an uncertain sound, they are to be blamed if sects come into being to bear more faithful witness to the biblical faith. The answer to this facet of the problem is for the churches to rediscover the relevance and transforming power of the mighty acts of God culminating in the Incarnation, the Cross, the Resurrection and the Second Coming of the eternal Son of God, by which the life of the church is renewed in the obedience of faith.

The church is always in need of reformation. The challenge of the sects is therefore best interpreted constructively as a summons to reformation. If the gospel is best commended by the church as a community of supernatural charity which condemns the chill and forbidding respectability of this world, then the fanaticism and missionary aggressiveness of the sects, as also their fervent devotion to the person of Christ, is a goad to awaken the church somnolent until it becomes again the church militant. As John Wesley found that the essence of Christian communication was one loving heart setting another afire, the churches must, in the final analysis, not only out-think but also out-love their opponents, the sectarians.

Even better would it be to avoid competition and to seek a genuine community of understanding at the grass roots level. At present there is too much isolation. As a result suspicion and misunderstanding of motives are rife.

NOTES

1. *World Christian Handbook* 1962, p.209.
2. See Geoffrey Moorhouse's article, 'Mormons in Britain'. *The Manchester Guardian Weekly*, 2 March 1962, p.12.
3. Statistics obtained from *The Yearbook of the American Churches*, 1971 ed.
4. Statistics obtained from *Christianity Today*, vol. 6, 19 December 1960, p.3.
5. Ibid., p.21.
6. Royston Pike, *Jehovah's Witnesses*, Watts, London and Philosophical Library, New York 1954, p.135.
7. See Elmer T. Clark, *The Small Sects in America*, rev. ed., Abingdon Press, New York and Nashville 1937, pp.219ff.
8. For a study of other 'independent' churches, see F. B. Welbourn, *East African Rebels*, SCM Press 1961; C. G. Baëta, *Prophetism in Ghana*, SCM Press 1962; Victor Hayward, *African Independent Church Movements*. Edinburgh House Press 1964.
9. Elmer T. Clark, op. cit., p.225.

FURTHER READING

Atkins, Gaius Glenn, *Modern Religious Cults and Movements*, Allen and Unwin, London, and Fleming Revell, New York 1923.

Black, James, *New Forms of the Old Faith*, Nelson, London 1948.

Braden, Charles S., *They Also Believe*, rev. ed., Macmillan Co., New York 1960.

Clark, Elmer T., *The Small Sects in America*, rev. ed., Abingdon Press, New York and Nashville 1937.

Gerstner, John, *The Theology of the Major Sects*, Baker, Grand Rapids, Michigan 1960.

Greenslade, S. L., *Schism in the Early Church*, rev. ed., SCM Press, London 1964.

Hoekema, Anthony, *The Four Major Cults*, Eerdmans, Grand Rapids, Michigan 1963.

Irvine, W. C., *Heresies Exposed*, Pickering and Inglis, 8th ed., London 1937.

Mathison, Richard, *Faiths, Cults and Sects of America, From Atheism to Zen*, Bobbs-Merrill Co., Indianapolis and New York 1960.

Mead, Frank S., *Handbook of Denominations in the United States*, Abingdon Press, New York and Nashville 1956.

Niebuhr, H. Richard, *The Social Sources of Denominationalism*, Meridian, New York 1957.

Radford, Lewis, *Ancient Heresies in Modern Dress*, Robertson, Melbourne 1913.

Ross, K. N., *Dangerous Delusions*, Mowbrays, London 1961.

Roy, Ralph Lord, *Apostles of Discord*, Beacon Press, Boston 1953.

Sanders, J. O., & Wright, J. S., *Some Modern Religions*, Tyndale Press, London 1956.

Sundkler, Bengt, *Bantu Prophets in South Africa*, Lutterworth Press, London 1948.

Van Baalen, J. K., *The Chaos of Cults*, Eerdmans, Grand Rapids, Michigan 1938.

Wilson, B. R., *Sects and Society: The Sociology of Three Religious Groups in Britain* (Elim Four Square Gospel Church, Christian Science, Christadelphians), Heinemann, London 1961.

2 The Jesus Freaks

But concerning love of the brethren
you have no need to have anyone write
to you, for you yourselves have been
taught by God how to love one
another ... (I Thessalonians 4.9)

Who are the Jesus Freaks?

This is the name given most commonly to those who were freaked out on marijuana or LSD and who are now freaked out on Jesus, that is, devotees of Jesus and enthusiastic disciples. They have given up their narcotic nirvana for the joy of Jesus.

This is the newest spiritual movement. It began in Sunset Strip, Los Angeles, in 1967, but has since spread to many cities in the United States, as also Europe. It is a movement no longer confined to reformed narcotic users, and the whole movement is now usually referred to as the 'Jesus Revolution' or the 'Jesus People'. Sometimes the converts are known as 'Street Christians', because they carry their witness to the streets in processions or in confrontation dialogues.

I

Most of them are easily identifiable as 'Jesus hippies' in appearance. They wear all the trappings of the counter-culture. Hair is long, beards are common. They wear beads around their necks, and bell-bottomed trousers are part of their uniform. They often read and deliver underground Christian papers. They are great fans of gospel-rock music, and they frequently live in Christian communes.

They have rediscovered Jesus as the great rebel against the establishment of his day, and therefore of these days. This feature of the movement was brilliantly brought out in the following advertisement that appeared recently in an underground Christian newspaper, depicting Jesus as an outlaw. It read as follows:

WANTED

JESUS CHRIST

ALIAS: THE MESSIAH, THE SON OF GOD,

KING OF KINGS, LORD OF LORDS, PRINCE OF PEACE, ETC.

—Notorious leader of an underground liberation movement:

—Wanted for the following charges:

... Practising medicine, wine-making and food distribution without a licence.

... Interfering with business in the temple.

... Associating with known criminals, radicals, subversives, prostitutes and street people.

... Claiming to have the authority to make people into God's children.

APPEARANCE: Typical hippie type – long hair, beard, robe, sandals.

... Hangs around slum areas, few rich friends, often sneaks out into the desert.

BEWARE: This man is extremely dangerous. His insidiously inflammatory message is particularly dangerous to young people who haven't been taught to ignore him yet. He changes men and claims to set them free.

WARNING: HE IS STILL AT LARGE.[1]

This is an identification with the Jesus who saw through the hypocrisy of the religious leaders of his day, who valued life above possessions and taught the supremacy of love and peace over hatred and war. Here is the clue to the enthusiasm of the Jesus revolution. This is not all of the mission or the message of Jesus of Nazareth, and it is far from the fullness of christology. Nonetheless, it is a new wave of the Spirit that is finding a quite extraordinary response in the youth of today.

II

The Jesus revolution has striking characteristics that distinguish it from other spiritual movements in recent times. Of basic importance is the fact that the movement is almost wholly *led and organized by students*. In many ways the current generation of students is the most daring, mature and responsible that has been seen in the English-speaking parts of the world. It is this age group (15-25) which has led the protest against war and racism. It is therefore not surprising that the same generation should be leading the Jesus movement, and with the fervour and imagination that youth can bring to any enterprise of pith and moment.

A second feature of the movement is its strong emphasis on caring for members of the *new community in Christ*. The term 'love' so often on the lips of these newest disciples is no mere catchword; it is a sincere conviction. Dr Donald Williams, one of the acutest observers of and participants in the movement, has commented: 'The false dichotomy of evangelical and social gospel does not exist on the personal level for these new Christians.'[2] A very remarkable facet of both hippiedom and the Jesus people is their support of communes. The hippie communes are supposed to practise free love, though that charge may well be exaggerated by the prurient and the suspicious, as well as the envious. The Christian communes, however, are free of the suspicion of moral laxity. Their inhabitants share all responsibilities in common. The girls are concerned with cleaning and cooking, while the boys take jobs or grow vegetables, being also responsible for decorating and maintaining the fabric of the houses in which the communes live. Each day special times are set aside for Bible-study and prayers. This communitarianism is deliberately evocative of the life of the apostolic church in which the earliest Christians, according to the record of the Acts of the Apostles, 'had all things common'. This is an impressive testimony to the depth of their fellowship and mutual concern.

The third feature of the new spiritual movement is an old one: its *biblicism*. The Bible is read as the living Word of God and the iron-rations of the soul. As will be mentioned later, some groups in the movement have made the New Testament into a new Leviticus – that is, they have introduced a new legalism into Christianity. This is particularly true of the group known as the 'Children of God'. They have renounced private property and normal employment to live totally celibate lives. They might be said, indeed, to have renounced private property, private thoughts and even private parts! They accept an imposed discipline of a military thoroughness and rigidity. They also voluntarily accept an unending mutual indoctrination.

The latter attitude is not, however, typical of the Jesus movement as a whole. They may rather be regarded as conservative evangelical Christians who, after the permissiveness of their upbringing, are delighted to accept absolute standards in belief and in behaviour. It gives them a bracing sense of security and a mission to convince others of the truth as they have found it in Christ.

A fourth feature is an *enterprising experimentation in outreach.* Some examples of this are exceedingly ingenious. There is, for example, a Jesus night-club. 'Right On' opened in Sunset Strip in July 1971, in a building that once was the scene of topless (and bottomless) shows and of female impersonators. 'With a dark wood bar (soft drinks only) and tables, red walls and carpeting, pool tables, and a door charge of $2.50 (£1 sterling), 'Right On' is designed to appeal to the young sophisticates who visit the Strip.'[3] Here Christian pop-singers and Christian rock-groups perform for the nightly audience.

Another type of experiment is holding Jesus festivals.[4] One such was held in Minneapolis in the summer of 1971, organized by Duane Pederson, publisher of the underground Christian paper, *The Hollywood Free Paper.* It gathered hundreds of young people together. It began with J-E-S-U-S ('Give me a J', etc.) cheers. A rock and very rhythmic version of 'O for a closer walk with Thee' was rousingly successful. The members of the crowd wore Jesus buttons inscribed 'Happiness is knowing Jesus'. At other rallies, youths are encouraged to clench their fists and point the index finger skyward, symbolizing 'one way in Christ'. All this is, of course, a modern adaptation of the techniques of revivalism, with a sophisticated use of modern advertising and a dash of crowd psychology.

The Jesus people have been particularly successful in employing the kind of post-jazz music that attracts youth. In fact, several stars in the popular music world are among their most notable converts. Perhaps the best known of these are Johnny Cash, Paul Stookey (of the trio Peter, Paul and Mary) and Jeremy Spencer of the Fleetwood Mac group. Pat Boone is a great supporter of the movement, and in 1971 more than 200 of the converts were baptized in his private swimming-pool.[5]

The ultimate triumphs of the new faith are to be found in the astonishingly successful musicals *Jesus Christ—Superstar* and the more biblically faithful *Godspell.*

Another experiment is the Jesus procession. Arthur Blessitt, a street evangelist, collected a crowd of 1,000 people in Grant Park, Chicago. After a Jesus cheer, he led them in a procession through the Loop (the central downtown part of the vast city of Chicago where the elevated railway loops between the skyscrapers). Gathering extra people as it went, the procession – instead of heckling the police, as is usual with demonstrators – shouted 'Chicago police, we love you.' They called to bystanders, 'Jesus loves you.' More interesting still, the leader passed a box through the crowd asking individuals to deposit any drugs they carried on their person in it. The box came back filled with marijuana, pills and LSD. It was then handed over to the amazed police.

Experimental ingenuity is also found in the establishment of communes. One such, the name of which symbolizes Christian security, is 'Solid Rock' of Novata, California. Drugs and pre-marital intercourse are rigidly prohibited. Duties are assigned and all must be abed by 10 or 11 p.m. Karsten Prager, a *Time* correspondent, who visited this Christian house or commune, reported: 'It is a gentle place this Solid Rock. The voices are quiet, the words that recur are "love" and "blessing" and "the Lord" and "sharing" and "peace" and "brothers and sisters". Twelve brothers and sisters live in Solid Rock, six men, four women, two babies – the children of unmarried mothers.' The correspondent added that the men of the commune work at house-painting and construction to meet the bills, but that 'the main business of the house is to order the lives within it around Christ'.[6]

At the beginning of this chapter an example was given of the ingenuity of the new Christian journalism in the movement, in the advertisement of Jesus as an outlaw still on the loose. The pro-liferation of a Christian underground press is yet another example of brilliant experimentation. These papers, paid for entirely by well-wishers and converts, are circulated free. They are as far away from the conventional parish magazine as it is possible to be. They employ cartoons, idiomatic speech and attention-getting tac-tics. Hundreds of thousands of copies (as in the case of the *Holly-wood Free Paper*) may be distributed, or only a few hundreds. The significant fact, however, is that there are now over fifty under-ground Christian papers in the USA.

The most impressive single book to have been promoted by the Jesus movement is the work of David Wilkerson, a minister of the theologically conservative Assemblies of God Church. He suc-ceeded in converting a vicious Brooklyn teenage street-gang leader or 'lord' by the name of Nicky Cruz in 1958. His book on this theme, *The Cross and the Switchblade*, has sold over six million copies. Incidentally, it has created an appreciation of Pentecostal fervour. The book has been made into a film, starring Pat Boone as Wilkerson.

In all these and in other ingenious ways the leaders of the Jesus people, following the example of St Paul, are 'being all things to all men, that they may save some'.

Perhaps the most impressive characteristic of the Jesus people, as their name implies, is their unbounded *admiration for Jesus of Nazareth*. What is the attraction of Jesus for the disillusioned members of the counter-culture?

Professor Martin Marty of the Chicago University Divinity School seems to think they are seeking a simplistic escape from the challenging complexities of our society. It is certainly likely that their apocalypticism may owe more to our contemporary culture than to the pages of the New Testament. There is good reason to despair over the stock-piling of hydrogen bombs, the dangers of over-population and the threats of universal pollution, which might easily lead to theological escapism. But this, of itself, does nothing to explain the attraction of the figure of Jesus.

Nor can it be explained in terms of the search by modern youth for a father figure who has an authority which presumably permissive parents have forfeited.

For all their simplistic attitude to Jesus (and frequent disregard of his divinity), there are significant points of contact between the historic Jesus and modern disenchanted members of the counter-culture. Such are: beards, sandals, a simple itinerant existence, the support and sharing of a group of friends or disciples. There are also deeper levels of agreement. The Jesus who is the prince of peace inevitably appeals to those disillusioned with the American involvement in the Vietnam war. The Jesus who accused the Pharisees and religious leaders of his day of being 'whited sepulchres' because of their hypocrisy, and because they preferred money and power to loving God and loving one's neighbours, finds resonance in these anti-establishment youths. The simplicity, love, peace and faith that Jesus preached and exemplified (and above all the fact that there is no gap between his profession and practice) appeal powerfully to the Jesus people.

III

It would be a mistake to assume that the Jesus revolution comprises essentially similar groups of people. In origin, as well as in composition, there are many different groups and associations included under the wide umbrella of the Jesus people.

Several different sparks and motivations helped to ignite the Jesus movement in California where it all began. The Christian World Liberation Front in Berkeley – that home of radical causes – aimed to provide an alternative to Marxism for those whose Christian consciences urged them to establish social justice. Calvary Chapel, with its concern for the renewal of Christian life among youth and its Pentecostalism, provided a church context for the newer revivalism. 'The Salt Company Coffee House' in Hollywood reached the present generation through its gospel-rock folk music. There was an authoritarian spark provided by the 'Jesus Army' in Seattle, Washington State. The student ministry at the University of California in Los Angeles in its 'Light and Power House' lit another flame. The hippies of the counter-culture helped by forming 'The Church in the Park' at Covina. One denomination helped through its lively programme on the media, 'Lutheran Youth Alive'. These many sparks or small flames helped to light the conflagration of the Jesus revolution.

Although the movement has many origins, its present development shows that it is maintained by four major groups.

The 'Jesus Freaks' or 'Street Christians' are probably the most visible group, and the majority of them affect the hippie style, though some gave it up on becoming Christians. They have blended the modality of the counter-culture with a conservative and even fundamentalistic type of religion. Nevertheless, this faith is not hardened by legalism or narrowed by cultural negativism. How could it be, indeed, if it were to hold youth who have been saturated with rock music, sex and drugs? As *Time*'s leading article on the phenomenon said : 'A good portion of the Movement is really a May-December marriage of conservative religion and the rebellious counter-culture, and many of the converts have come to Christ from the fraudulent promises of drugs.'[7]

A second group can most conveniently be called the 'Straight People'. These constitute the largest group by far. They are active in interdenominational youth and campus movements in the United States and correspond very much to the Inter-Varsity Fellowship Christians in Britain. Once they seemed to be an arm of evangelical Protestantism. Now, however, they seem to be more ecumenical in outlook. In appearance they are Middle American. Their short hair is neatly cut and combed, and they wear standard or bourgeois clothes. In the youth idiom they are impressive 'squares'.

A third and unusual group is that of the 'Catholic Pentecostals'. While loyal to the Roman Catholic church, they are unsettling to its hierarchy. They react negatively to the authoritarianism, impersonality and triumphalism of the bureaucracy of their church. They find the spontaneity of worship, closeness of fellowship and, above all, the fervour and dynamism of the Holy Spirit in the Pentecostalist movement a necessary ecstatic supplement to their Catholicism. This sub-sect began in Duquesne University in 1967 and later spread to Notre Dame University and then on to the University of Michigan. In July 1971 no less than three thousand Catholic Pentecostalists convened at Notre Dame for an annual conference. This interesting movement is meeting some heavy Catholic crossfire – their orthodoxy in doctrine alienates Catholic liberals, and their speaking with tongues and community life alienates the Catholic conservatives. But they are a vigorous group.

The strangest of the groups is known as the Children of God. This is a quasi-military and even (despite its Protestant matrix) a quasi-monastic movement. Like monks, its novices cut their hair (their 'tonsure'). They also make strict vows of chastity, poverty and obedience. But, unlike Catholic monks or nuns, they give up all hope for contemporary culture or social betterment.

IV

What should be the attitude of members of the mainstream churches towards the Jesus revolution? In brief, the answer is: a combination of genuine encouragement and also of watchfulness.

There is strong ground for encouragement in the enthusiasm, the experimentation, the close fellowship and the return to the values of peace and love so strikingly exhibited by the Jesus people. In all these respects they are the most hopeful allies the mainstream of Christianity has received in the present century.

In several respects they have much to teach the churches, if only the latter will be sympathetic. They point, in the first place, to a new way of acknowledging the primacy of Christ in life. They show that modern youth is less attracted by the demands of dogmatic or doctrinal assent than by the style and conduct of a leader who is original and irresistible. As Professor Doris Donnelly, a perceptive Catholic theologian on the Fordham University faculty, has expressed it: 'The Jesus of the Gospels unadorned by metaphysical speculation and conciliar formulae is the one worthy of total allegiance, the one because of whom any number of young people can say, with Mary Magdalene of *Jesus Christ—Superstar*, "I've been changed; yes, really changed".[8] The earliest christology of the New Testament began with a response to the man Jesus, as can be seen in the Acts of the Apostles. The method is to proceed from Jesus to the Christ, through the humanity to the divinity, and not *vice versa*.

The Jesus People are also a very effective reminder that no institution (not even the most venerable and largest) has an exclusive monopoly on Jesus or his Spirit. In our time again we see that the Holy Spirit, like the invisible wind, blows where he wills. On the part of the institutional churches a new openness of heart will be required to recognize and appreciate an admiration for Jesus in unaccustomed ways and in unexpected quarters. Above all, the churches must be grateful for the exuberance and contagion of the Jesus people.

Nonetheless, there is also room for second thoughts and some serious misgivings. True friends of the Jesus people must point out to them their dangerous preference for subjectivity (or experience) over history which leads them to dilute and distort the historic Christian faith. As George Santayana once put it, 'those who do not know the past are doomed to relive it'. The particular nature of the weakness is the tendency to adopt what appeals to them in Jesus and to ignore the rest. This subjectivity takes the form of viewing Jesus as the first hippie and anti-establishment hero, as well as a progenitor of the feeling-encounter experience. The great disadvantage of this approach to Jesus is that it forgets the 'hard sayings' of the Master, such as, 'If any man would follow me, let him take up his cross.' There is in the Jesus movement a sense of fellowship with Jesus in his joy, but none of sharing, with St Paul, in 'the fellowship of Christ's sufferings'. The gospel makes demands, as well as offering delights.

Furthermore, the biblicism of the Jesus people is both absolutist and all-too-simple. It is too convenient to use the scriptures as an armoury of proof-texts, for proof-texts apart from their contexts become only pretexts. A reporter who was very sympathetic to the Jesus freaks described them 'as scoring points with scriptural quotations' rather than answering his questions with rational and relevant replies. He thus describes his frustrating experience in dialogue with them: 'Mention that a personal God seems a mighty difficult concept to carry in this age of electronic holocaust and thermonuclear despair and you get a quote from Matthew about how you first seek the Kingdom of God and everything else will fall into place. Point out how the churches of Jesus seem to work hand in glove with the very people who seem to be oppressing the people of God, and you get the old "whited-sepulchre" bit as an answer.'[9] Citation of scripture, without explanation and justification, is no substitute for thought.

Finally, as one recalls the virtual disappearance or growing irrelevance of other recent American religious enthusiasms, such as Muslims, Panthers and Zen, one is forced to ask whether the Jesus revolution has staying power or is only a passing fad. Only time can provide that answer, but in the interim one may note certain promising signs presaging that it is more than a transient phenomenon. It is a movement of great variety that cuts across all social divisions, from rich to poor, from long hair to crew cut. One might judge its staying power from the fact that many of those who were in the movement at its beginning in 1967 are still in it. Furthermore, it has an ecumenical appeal, attractive to both Roman Catholics and to Protestants of all varieties. Perhaps its most promising feature of all is the movement's proven power to transform drug users into disciples of Christ. Such power should never be underestimated.

NOTES

1. In the article 'The New Rebel Cry: Jesus is Coming', *Time*, 21 June 1971, pp.56-63.

2. 'Close-up of the Jesus People', *Christianity Today*, 27 August 1971, p.6.

3. News item in *Christianity Today*, 6 August 1971, p.37.

4. See Anne Eggebroten's article, ibid., pp.38f.

5. *Time*, 21 June 1971, p.61.

6. Ibid., p.62.

7. Ibid., p.59.

8. 'Jesus and the Star System', *America*, 30 October 1971, p.350.

9. Phil Tracy, 'The Jesus Freaks: Savagery and Salvation on Sunset Strip', *Commonweal*, 30 October 1970, pp.123f.

FURTHER READING

Roger C. Palms, *The Jesus Kids*, Judson Press, Valley Forge, 1971, and SCM Press, London 1972.

3   The Seventh-Day Adventists

Now therefore why tempt ye God, that
ye should put a yoke upon the neck of
the disciples, which neither we nor
our fathers were able to bear?
(Acts 15.10)

One of the most attractive religious groups, bearing a close resemblance to Protestantism, is that of the Seventh-Day Adventists. They arose from the vast millenarian hopes of the disinherited who flourished in the middle decades of the nineteenth century in America (like the Mormons). Formally organized in 1863, they numbered only 4,000 in 1865, but just over a hundred years later they are active in 189 countries of the world, and number over a million and a half members. In the USA their membership, according to the 1971 edition of *The Yearbook of the American Churches,* was 407,766.

Theirs is not a startling, but it is a steady progress. How is it to be accounted for? Unquestionably it is due largely to the thoroughness with which this religious community devotes itself to its ideals.

One is first of all impressed by their generosity. Not only is every Seventh-Day Adventist expected to give a tenth of his or her income before deduction of taxes, but many also give a further tithe of their income to support the impressive programmes of their church for missionary, welfare, educational, medical and publishing work. Economically it should be recalled that the Adventists fall into the middle or lower-middle classes. This is therefore in the strictest sense costly and sacrificial giving.

A second factor helping to account for their success is their serious and sustained commitment to the improvement of physical health. No religious group in the world can compare with their record in this respect. In 1964, for example, they treated 3,850,000 patients (that is, over ten times the number of their US membership) in the 124 Advent hospitals and 146 clinics and treatment-rooms. On a world-wide basis they employ over 500 Doctors of Medicine, the vast majority of whom were trained at their highly-regarded medical centre at Loma Linda University in Southern California. It is here that not only physicians, but also dentists and medical technologists are prepared for their careers.

The same concern for health has characterized them from earliest days, for they have been specially interested in preventive medicine. It was an Adventist layman, Dr J. H. Kellogg, who invented cornflakes and changed the heavy (bacon and eggs) break-fast of a nation into the lighter repast now most common. Seventh-Day Adventists have always insisted on total abstinence from hard liquor, tobacco and narcotics. For health reasons the majority of Adventists have become vegetarians, and even those who are not vegetarians observe prohibitions against eating pork, ham and shellfish.

Thirdly, the Adventists are remarkable in their commitment to education. Like Catholics, they have embarked on a scheme to prevent their youth from the scepticism of secular education by providing Adventist parochial schools and colleges at considerable cost to the denomination. In the United States in 1965 they had 5,074 schools with 342,472 pupils from kindergarten to collegiate levels of instruction. In the United States alone they support two universities, ten liberal arts colleges and two junior colleges. A comparison will show their high level of educational responsibility: the Protestant Episcopal Church, ten times the size of the Advent-ists in membership, supports fewer colleges than the Adventists. So eager are they to shoulder their educational responsibilities that they will open a grade school if there are as few as twenty pupils to start it.

In the fourth place, this denomination does not leave witnessing only to the professionals, the clergy. On the contrary, by the use of effective Bible schools and the high level of expectation that every Adventist will be able to give a reason for the faith he holds, they have a veritable army of aggressive evangelists.

Fifthly and finally, some are unquestionably attracted by their distinctive beliefs. Even their Adventism, with its conviction of the imminence of the Second Coming of Jesus Christ, does represent a protest against the modernism that teaches an inevitable pro-gress towards Utopia – a view that is increasingly dated by the threats of modern life, and the less refined traditionalism that clings to a belief in a hell where the damned suffer everlasting torments. In opposition to both these concepts, Seventh-Day Adventism declares that the Second Advent will take place quietly (that is, no blood-curdling Armageddon will bring the new world-order in) and that evil-doers will be annihilated, not subjected to eternal tortures. At least God is reprieved from the charge of masochism and the faithful from the charge of gloating over the miseries of others.

I

The movement can only be understood if a brief account of its history is given. As in the case of Christian Science and also of Theosophy, Seventh-Day Adventists had a female founder, Ellen Harmon, although she is better known under her married name, as Mrs Ellen White. Just as Mrs Baker Eddy leaned heavily upon the teaching and practice of Quimby, Mrs White made much use of the ideas of William Miller, founder of the original Adventists.

William Miller was a Baptist, born at Pittsfield, Massachusetts, in 1782, and who was educated at Low Hampton in New York State. This honest farmer was a great student of the Bible (though without any knowledge of historical criticism). In 1831 he announced that he had discovered the exact date of Christ's Second Coming. He was most sanguine in declaring that on the basis of the predictions of the books of Daniel and Revelation, this event would take place in 1843. When nothing happened in 1843, he admitted a mistake in his calculations and postponed the fulfilment of his prophecy until the following year. When he was proved wrong a second time, he gave up Adventism. In his very significant statement of renunciation he stated:

> On the passing of the published time, I frankly acknowledge my disappointment. We expected the personal coming of Christ at that time; and now to contend that we were not mistaken is dishonest. We should never be ashamed frankly to confess our errors. I have no confidence in any of the new theories that grew out of that movement, namely, that Christ then came as the Bridegroom, that the door of mercy was closed, that there is no salvation for sinners, that the seventh trumpet then sounded, or that it was a fulfilment of prophecy in any sense.[1]

Despite this exceedingly honest recantation of Miller, Ellen Harmon (White), an intense young woman, persisted in believing that Miller's prophecies were substantially correct. As a result she

founded a movement which was named the Seventh-Day Adventists. The members of the new group held the view that 'the Lord
did really come in 1844, not to earth, but to cleanse the sanctuary in Heaven ... The Lord passed into the sanctuary in 1844,
which Mrs White was taken up to heaven and shown.'[2]

They believed that Christ first cleansed the sanctuary and began
the final judgment, closing the door of mercy to sinners. They
claimed that only those in the know about this 'change' could
benefit by Christ's mediation. According to Ellen White, others
only 'offer up their useless prayers to the apartment which Jesus
left'.[3] Thus it seems, in the origin of the Adventists, salvation was
made to depend on knowledge of an event of 1844 of which Adventists alone had heard. Their name also implies that they lay great
stress on the *seventh-day* sabbath, the day on which God rested
after completing his creation. They regard other Christians who
changed the sabbath in honour of the Resurrection of Jesus Christ
to the first day of the week as bearing the 'mark of the beast'. Their
distinctive claims are that they alone preach the three messages
referred to in Revelation 14.6-12, that 'the seal of God is the holy
sabbath' and that the 144,000 to be translated at the Second Advent
are now being 'sealed'.

II

The unique beliefs of the Seventh-Day Adventists must now be
treated in greater detail. Their first feature is, of course, their
teaching on Adventism. It should, of course, be stated to avoid
misunderstanding that they accept the scriptures of the Old and
New Testaments as authoritative for their understanding of Christian doctrine. As we have seen, although the first founder of the
Adventist movement, William Miller, admitted that his Advent predictions had been erroneous, Mrs White refused to give up either
the idea or the second date of the predicted Second Advent of
Christ.

Mrs White was able to give a significance to the year 1844 by the
assertion that Christ entered into the sanctuary of heaven to effect
its cleansing in that year. This statement was made, however,
through what the historic Christian churches could only describe
as a distortion of the New Testament teaching on the atonement.
Mrs White held that the work of Christ was not finished on earth
in the days of his passion, because 'as the closing portion of his
work as priest, before he takes his throne as King, he will make the

great atonement'.[4] According to her, Christ entered only the outer sanctuary, not the holy of holies, at his Ascension, although this seems to be contradicted by Hebrews 1.3.

Another very prominent feature in Adventist teaching is the insistence upon a seventh-day sabbath. This position is defended on biblical and historical grounds. While Mrs Ellen White acknowledged that the new covenant of Jesus Christ had abrogated the old dispensation of Moses, she yet held that the moral, as contrasted with the ceremonial, precepts of the Law were still binding on every Christian. She went on to insist that, since the observance of the seventh day occurs as one of the commandments of the moral law, therefore the observance of the sabbath on the seventh day is unrepealed. It is therefore of perpetual obligation for Christians. To substantiate this teaching Mrs White claimed to have had a vision of the sanctuary in heaven where

> Jesus raised the cover of the ark, and she beheld the tables of stone on which the ten commandments were written. She was amazed as she saw the Fourth Commandment in the very centre of the ten precepts, with a soft halo of light encircling it.[5]

The historical claim of the Seventh-Day Adventists that the churches fell into apostasy in this matter rests on the assertion that the Council of Laodicea in AD 364 changed the sabbath or seventh day to Sunday or the first day of the week.

What is perhaps of greater value is to understand how the Adventists in fact spend their sabbath. For devout Adventists, as for Jews, the sabbath begins at sunset on a Friday. Meals are prepared on Friday so that the housewife need not be bothered with them on the sabbath. Saturday morning is spent in church and sabbath school. The remainder of the day is devoted to the reading and study of the Bible, discussing religious topics with friends and simple family recreations such as nature walks. Both the radio and television are turned off throughout the sabbath day until it ends at sundown on Saturday. In the creative use of their sabbath, the Adventists have an example to offer to traditional Christians, who may make a nod – no more – to the Sunday by attending church and then ignoring God for the rest of the day.

The Adventists teach that Jesus inherited a fallen human nature, as may be gathered from the following citation:

> In his humanity Christ partook of our sinful, fallen nature. If not, then he was not 'made like unto us his brethren', was

not 'in all points tempted like as we are', did not overcome as we have to overcome, and is not therefore the complete and perfect Saviour man needs and must have to be saved.[6]

Their final distinctive teaching is their belief in the sleep of the soul after death. The state of the dead is said to be 'one of silence, inactivity and entire unconsciousness'. The five proof-texts for this doctrine, all significantly taken from the Old Testament and not from the New, are: Psalm 146.4; Ecclesiastes 9.5,6,10; Daniel 12.2.

III

The beliefs of Seventh-Day Adventists deserve careful attention, partly because so much of their general teaching is close to that of evangelical Christianity, and also because they are an expanding religious community.

Their insistence upon keeping the seventh day, or Jewish sabbath, in contradistinction to the rest of Christendom, and their delineation of those who keep Sunday as a special day as exhibiting the 'mark of the beast' is not only a denial of charity, but smacks of a legalism foreign to the dominant spirit of the New Testament.

St Paul in Colossians 2.14 rightly reminds us that the 'handwriting of ordinances' (the Law of Moses) was 'blotted out' and nailed to the Cross, as in ancient times old bills were nailed to the doorpost when paid off. Since Christ, so Christians believe, has met every claim of the Law, its precepts are no longer obligatory on Christians. The distinction which Mrs Ellen White made between ceremonial and moral law is unknown in the Old Testament, as a perusal of Exodus 24.3 will convincingly demonstrate. Further, it is very difficult to understand how she could have regarded the observance of a particular day as more holy or fitting than another as a moral issue, when it is more clearly one of ceremonial import. In any case, members of the historic Christian churches are supposed to believe in the supremacy of grace over law, whereas she would make the New Testament a new Leviticus. The New Testament shows that even the moral law of the Old Testament is superseded. The Old Testament declares, 'Thou shalt not kill.' But this negative precept is replaced in the New Testament by the more positive, penetrating and comprehensive counsel, 'If thine enemy hunger, feed him; if he thirst, give him drink.'

The grace of Christ frees Christians from empty ceremonial and scrupulous adherence to the letter of the Law. St Augustine insisted that the ethical precepts of Christianity could be summed up in the injunction: 'Love God and do what you like.' In brief, this doctrine of the Seventh-Day Adventists appears to be an irrelevant legalism in the life of the Spirit. It is already condemned in the words of Colossians 2.16-17: 'Let no man therefore judge you in meat or in drink or in respect of an holy day, or of the new moon, or of the sabbath days, which are a shadow of things to come; but the body is of Christ.'

There is, moreover, a positive reason for the change from the seventh day to the first for the celebration of the Lord's Day in the Christian dispensation. The old sabbath was a memorial of the origin of life in the creation of the world; the new sabbath or Sunday, commemorating the Resurrection of Christ, is a memorial of the victory of life over death. In the felicitous words of Dr Lewis Radford:

> The old Sabbath marked the close of the first stage of divine activity, Creation; the new Lord's Day marks the beginning of the second stage, Regeneration. The Sabbath ended the week with the *Nunc Dimittis* of resignation; the Lord's Day begins the week with a *Te Deum* of renewal.[7]

Even the claim that the Council of Laodicea introduced the change from Jewish sabbath to Christian is a misleading one. In the first place, this was an Eastern council and it was not binding on the more important Western churches. In the second place, it merely forbade Christians to abstain from work on the Jewish sabbath, calling this practice 'Judaizing'. In fact, there is evidence to show that the Lord's Day was generally celebrated on the first day of the week in the second century. The early second-century *Epistle to Barnabas* records: 'Wherefore, also, we keep the eighth day with joyfulness, the day also on which Jesus rose from the dead.' And Justin Martyr, writing about the middle of the second century, declares: 'But Sunday is the day on which we all hold a common assembly, because it is the first day of the week on which God ... made the world; and Jesus Christ our Saviour on the same day rose from the dead.'

Next we must consider the Adventism of the movement. Certainly the New Testament and the Apostles' Creed both insist on the Second Coming as a basic article of belief. But the Seventh-Day Adventists go beyond the statement of Christ, who claimed of the date of the Second Advent, 'No man knoweth the hour, not even the Son'. Their early history could certainly be charged with wanting to know more than had been vouchsafed to the Messiah himself.

It seems to me legitimate to argue that the doctrine of the sanctuary held and expounded by the Adventists would destroy the true meaning of the Ascension of Christ and his priesthood. They claim that there were two stages in Christ's high priesthood, corresponding to the Jewish high priest's ministrations first in the outer chamber and then in the inner chamber of the earthly tabernacle. But the Epistle to the Hebrews (9.24) represents Jesus as entering into the inmost sanctuary of the presence of God, not merely to purify the heavenly things, but 'now to appear before the face of God for us'. In the New Testament, purifying and appearing are clearly but two aspects of the same fact. Adventists have, therefore, no shred of biblical evidence for their fantastic belief that the appearance of the perfect man to present his sacrifice of obedience even unto death took place in AD 1844. The writer of Hebrews (8.1) believed that it took place at Christ's Ascension. The logical consequences of this belief, with its denial of the New Testament assurance that Christ 'ever liveth to make intercession for us', are drawn by Dr Radford in the following comment:

Adventism stands committed to the amazing theory that for eighteen centuries the ascended Christ was still waiting to enter the sanctuary of the presence of God and to prepare the heavenly world for the approach of man to God ... If this atoning entry took place in 1844, what was the scene, the character, the efficacy of His activity for those eighteen centuries of human time?[8]

The effect of this belief is also to reduce the function of the Holy Spirit during eighteen centuries to being the minister of the unfinished work of the Father and the Son.

What are we to think of the Adventists' assertion that the intermediate state after death is one of complete unconsciousness? As we have seen, there are several Old Testament texts that will serve as warrants for such a belief. The New Testament, however, teaches directly or by implication that the soul in the unseen world is fully conscious, though some references also imply that Christians are sleeping in the intermediate state. At any rate the following references all imply the full consciousness of the soul after death: the parable of Lazarus (Luke 16.22-25); Christ's promise to the dying thief (Luke 23.43); the impatient cry of the waiting martyrs (Revelation 6.9-11); and the earnest wish of St Paul (Philippians 1.21) and the missionary activity of the human spirit of the Christ among the departed between his death and his resurrection (I Peter 3.19 and 4.6) raise serious questions about the dogmatic assertion of the Adventists that souls are unconscious after death.

When the entire series of doctrinal deviations of the Adventists is considered, and even allowing for the curious assertion that Christ's work was not completed until 1844, they are in faith and especially in the fruits of faith extremely close to the Protestant wing of Christianity. They add no other scriptures to those accepted by the historic churches. They affirm their belief in the Holy Trinity. They believe in the divinity of Jesus Christ and that he is the saviour of the world. They assert the primacy of faith over works. They are men and women who are proud to be Bible Christians. And their millenarianism has not in the least prevented them from giving notable service to mankind through their hospitals. These are potential allies, not foes of the historic Christian churches!

NOTES

1. *History of the Advent Message*, pp.410f.
2. *Early Writings*, pp.114f.
3. *Spiritual Gifts*, p.172.
4. *Fundamental Principles*.
5. Cited by W. C. Irvine, *Heresies Exposed*, Pickering and Inglis, 8th ed., London 1937, p.149.
6. *Bible Readings for the Home Circle*, 1915. ed., p.115.
7. Lewis Radford, *Ancient Heresies in Modern Dress*, Robertson, Melbourne 1913, p.78.
8. Ibid., p.87.

FURTHER READING

Froom, L. R. E., *The Prophetic Faith of Our Fathers*, 4 vols., Washington, DC, 1946-54.

Olsen, M. E., *A History of the Origin and Progress of the Seventh-Day Adventists*, Washington, DC, 3rd ed., 1932.

Maxwell, A. S., *Your Friends the Adventists*, Pacific Press Publishing Assoc., Mountain View, California 1960.

CRITIQUES

Bird, Herbert S., *Theology of Seventh-Day Adventism*, Eerdmans, Grand Rapids, Michigan 1961.

Mitchell, David, *Seventh-Day Adventists: Faith in Action*, Vantage Press, New York 1958 — a sympathetic account by a non-Adventist.

4 Christian Science

Who in the days of his flesh, having
offered up prayers and supplications
with strong crying and tears ... though
he was a Son, yet learned obedience
by the things which he suffered
(Hebrews 5.7-8)

The outward signs of Christian Science are two: quiet reading-rooms in the busy thoroughfares of cities and towns, and elegant, well-proportioned Georgian churches of redbrick and white painted wood, both redolent of New England. The founder of Christian Science was Mary Baker Eddy, entirely the product of New England culture. Born into a New Hampshire family, she was brought up in the historic and dominant church of that area, Congregationalism, and she responded positively to the romantic idealism of New England associated with R. W. Emerson and his colleagues, which was known as Transcendentalism. Her life's work was exercised in the stimulating confines of New England and, not surprisingly, Boston – the hub of all that culture – is the headquarters of the Church of Christ, Scientist, and the home of the mother church.

Christian Science bears so evidently the impact and impress of Mrs Eddy that it cannot be understood apart from the odyssey of the remarkable lady who was its founder. She was born in Bow, New Hampshire, in 1821, the sixth child of a gentleman-farmer and his wife. Both parents were respected members of the local Congregational church. A highly sensitive and conscientious child, she reacted strongly against the stern and forbidding Calvinism of her father's creed. Her later teaching, which was compounded of many elements of thought and practice, was partly formulated in antagonism to Calvinism's assertion that trials and sorrows are inevitable since they are sent by God for the spiritual steeling and strengthening of his children. During much of her childhood, she was subject to a serious nervous illness which continued through many years of adulthood. Unfortunately for her, both her father and her first husband seemed to think she was a hypochondriac and had little sympathy for her sickness. Her first husband was a building contractor, whose vast profits were largely contributed by the exploitation of the slaves he owned. Soon after the marriage, he died of yellow fever, leaving her with a small son and considerable assets, which were employed in freeing the slaves and in educating her child. The young widow then married a dentist, by name Dr Patterson. So enfeebled was she at this time, that Patterson had to carry her downstairs from her bedroom for the ceremony of marriage and carry her back again there on its completion. Eventually he turned out to be a scapegrace, who became infatuated with other women, and abandoned her. She had to bring up her ailing child alone. Patterson did, however, perform one good turn for his wife, by introducing her to a dynamic but unorthodox healer, Phineas P. Quimby, who was able to provide her with some of the practical hints upon which she was to build up the practice (if not the theory and metaphysics) of Christian Science.[1] He claimed there was only one cure for all diseases – the confidence of the patient in the healer, and he was a pioneer of the mental healing of diseases. Mary Baker Eddy, however, as will be seen, always subordinated mental techniques to their spiritual ends, a concern which was lacking in Quimby.

Quimby described his healing art in the following manner: 'My practice,' he said, 'is unlike all medical practice. I give no medicine, and make no outward applications. I tell the patient his troubles, and that's what he thinks is his disease, and my explanation is the cure. If I succeed in correcting his errors, I change the fluids of the system, and establish the patient in health. The truth is the cure.' Mrs Eddy's indebtedness to Quimby is perhaps greater than either Mrs Eddy or the Christian Scientists have been prepared to admit. His manuscripts, since published, show that he referred to his mind-healing system as Christian Science and that he called disease an error. He wrote: 'Disease is false reasoning. False reasoning is sickness and death.' This might well be considered the central tenet of Christian Science as elaborated by Mrs Eddy. By implication, she denied any borrowings, for her compendium of Christian Science contains the claim: 'No human pen or tongue taught me the science contained in the book.'[2]

In October 1862, Mary Baker Patterson (as she then was) presented herself to Phineas P. Quimby at the International Hotel, Portland, Maine. He informed her that her animal spirit was reflecting its grief upon her body, and calling it spinal disease. He then dipped his hands in water, rubbed her head violently, and sent her into a mesmeric sleep. When she awoke, her pain had disappeared. The cure seemed to be as complete as it was quick. Nor was there any relapse. She explained to Quimby that her disease was cured by the healer's understanding of the truth of Christ brought by him into the world and lost for centuries, and not by Quimby's mesmerism. Quimby, an unbeliever, utterly denied the explanation. His patient, however, refused to accept his disclaimer, and was so far restored to health that she mounted the hundred and eighty-two steps to the Dome of Portland City Hall to advertise to the world the greatness of Quimby. Most significant in this incident is the attribution of the healing to God. This is the basis of *Christian* Science, rather than the use of non-physical modes of treatment. The development of the theory of Christian Science and its vivid expression is the distinctive contribution of Mary Baker Eddy.

She spent the next two years lecturing on Quimby's cures and in trying to Christianize them by writing interpolated interpretations in his case-book. Meanwhile Quimby died of an ulcer in the stomach in 1866, which is also the year given for the foundation of Christian Science.

She began the Christian Science movement by treating private patients and by lecturing on the art of faith-healing. In 1875 there appeared the first of many editions of her world-famous handbook *Science and Health*. Two years later Mary Baker Patterson became Mary Baker Eddy by marrying Asa Gilbert Eddy, an able businessman, congenial agent for a firm of manufacturers of sewing-machines. He saw to it that the second and third editions of his wife's handbook were protected from literary piracy, thus safeguarding the copyright and the considerable profits from the work. Mrs Eddy was also introduced by her husband to influential persons in Boston, where she lectured. Her husband was her devoted missionary. Over 3,200 churches and organizations in the world now acknowledge her as their spiritual leader. She founded a college in which Christian Scientists would be trained, a famous newspaper (*The Christian Science Monitor*), and an international religious organization.

She proved herself to be a woman of high administrative ability, a clear and dynamic as well as charming lecturer. Her logical and speculative abilities were of a high order, and she had a gift for lucid and occasionally vivid expression. Her greatest quality was her empathy and determination to help to heal the sorrows and ills of mankind. She rediscovered and expressed in her own character the radiance that should be the distinctive mark of the Christian life. This frail lady was an astonishing example of the triumph of the spirit over matter until her death from pneumonia in 1910 at the age of eighty-nine. Christian Science now has an estimated world membership of 367,000.[3]

I

What was the key to her success and what were the benefits of her popular system? Unquestionably, she gave a new sense of well-being to multitudes of neurotic and depressed persons. She radiated confidence, and thousands of fearful, melancholy and self-pitying hypochondriacs learned from her how to be robustly cheerful with a faith to live by. In a materialistic age she inculcated a belief in a spiritual interpretation of life, and she rediscovered the Christian art of faith-healing.

For a considerable time the notes of happiness and health had been missing from the Christian symphony. Mary Baker Eddy taught that conformity to the will of God, as taught by Christ, was the very wellspring of human happiness, but that it had to be founded also upon good health.

In the third place, she brought back to many Protestants a forgotten discipline – the regular, daily meditation upon a passage of the Bible, together with a prescribed section of her *Science and Health*. This put order into chaotic lives and significance into lives that previously had suffered from meaninglessness.

Fourthly, she repudiated notions of God that were unworthy, however popular. In particular, she criticized the idea that all pain is imposed by God to teach his children resignation. She propagated a belief in the absolute goodness of God. In fact, she propagated it so profoundly that she met the age-old problem of evil in a divinely created universe by denying its reality.

Fifthly, and very importantly, she showed by her own contribution the significant role that women can play in organized religion. While Roman Catholicism has given to its mothers superior and to its saints (like Theresa of Avila) significant roles, they have never been commensurate with the numbers of their adherents. In Protestantism (since the role of the Virgin is considerably lower than in Catholicism), it is only since the time of Mrs Eddy that women have been ordained in some denominations.

The recognition of this debt that Christianity owes to women has undoubtedly been a factor accounting for the success of Christian Science. Mrs Eddy was a 'woman's liberationist' long before the term was employed.

In fact, it was her restoration of spiritual healing and of the eminently responsible role of women to Christianity that constitute her chief claims to fame and appreciation.

II

What were the essential tenets of her thought? These can be found in two of her own summaries. One of them is used in every Christian Science service, and is memorized by every Christian Scientist, a proof of its central significance as a *credo*. It reads thus:

> There is no life, truth, intelligence, nor substance in matter. All is infinite Mind and its infinite manifestation, for God is All-in-all. Spirit is the real and eternal; matter is the unreal and temporal. Spirit is God, and man is His image and likeness. Therefore man is not material; he is spiritual.[4]

The author has also summarized her beliefs in another place, which reads:

First. God is all in all.
Second. God is Good. Good is mind.
Third. God, Spirit being all, nothing is matter.
Fourth. Life, God, omnipotent, good, deny death, evil, sin, disease. – Disease, sin, evil, death, deny good, omnipotent, God, Life.[5]

It will be immediately apparent that her system *appears* to rest on four categorical denials. She seems to deny the existence of matter, pain, evil and death: at the very least she stresses their unreality in any fundamental sense. The difficult thought that though unreal their false reality can have serious mental effects does not make it easier to understand Mrs Eddy. Her specific view of sickness states that: 'Sickness is neither imaginary nor unreal – that is, to the frightened, false sense of the patient. Sickness is more than fancy; it is solid conviction. It is therefore to be dealt with through right apprehension of the truth of being.'[6] It is, of course, one thing to say that matter is not eternal; it is quite another to deny its ultimate reality. At the very outset it makes absurd the central Christian doctrine that the Word of God became *flesh* and dwelt among us. Why was Mrs Eddy prompted to make this denial, contrary to all human experience? (It may be remembered that Dr Samuel Johnson rejected the extreme form of Berkeley's assertion of the non-existence of matter by striking his foot against a large stone, till he rebounded from it, saying, 'I refute it *thus*'.) Perhaps she thought that the body was the source of all evil; but this is not so. It is the imagination and will that are sources of sinfulness. For the Christian, matter is not evil, but rather its misuse. Indeed, the Christian recalls that, according to the Book of Genesis, when God had created the material world, he declared it to be *good*.

In the second place, Mrs Eddy denies the ultimate reality of pain and sickness. Pain and suffering depend on our foolish belief in the reality of matter, according to her. She goes so far as to assert: 'A child may have worms, *if you say so*, or any other malady.' She further avers that: 'The boil simply manifests through inflammation and swelling a belief in pain, and this belief is called a boil.'[7] The only appropriate response is to ask how one can poultice a *belief*, or to recite the limerick:

> There was a faith-healer of Deal,
> Who said, 'Although pain isn't real,
>   When I sit on a pin
>   which punctures my skin,
> I dislike what I fancy I feel.'

The limerick does not, however, hide the fact that a great deal of modern medicine acknowledges the point that Mrs Eddy is making, namely, that many illnesses demonstrate the interdependence of mind and body, and are psychosomatic sicknesses. But when that fact is granted, as it must be, it is going too far to assert that pain in all its forms is sheer illusion. The heart of the Christian gospel is that we have a suffering saviour and that by faith in him we are able to transform suffering into blessing, sin into righteousness, and death into eternal life. Our faith is built upon that strange man who hangs upon the cross. It seems pertinent to ask: how *Christian* can a faith be which denies the reality of the cross, the very centre and sign of historic Christianity? As H. A. L. Fisher says, in the conclusion of *Our New Religion*: 'For the Christian Scientist a brilliant pioneer of drugless healing ... replaces the suffering figure on the Cross.'

In the third place, Mrs Eddy denies the reality of evil and sin. She declares: 'Both sin and sickness are error, and Truth is their remedy.'[8] This denial issues from an honourable determination to 'justify the ways of God to man'. She preserves the unassailable goodness of God by the expedient of denying the existence of evil and sin. However, to assert that sin does not exist, except as an illusion, is virtually to deny the saving work of Christ and to make his death (as his sufferings) mere phantasms. On the hypothesis of the Christian Scientists, Jesus laboured under the 'delusion' that sin was a reality. Either Jesus' desire to redeem mankind and obtain forgiveness for their sins was an error, or, at the very least, he came only to prove that our belief in sin was mistaken. In fact, however, the realism of the Christian faith enables us to come to grips with the demonic power of evil by the example of Jesus Christ and in the power of the Holy Spirit.

Fourthly, the existence of death is denied. Mrs Eddy asserts: 'Life is real and death is the illusion.' Her reasoning seems to be that since we are essentially spiritual and the matter of our bodies is illusory, there is nothing of us that can die. This claim, of course, is in open contradiction to the Christian faith which is born out of the Easter forgiveness, when death was rather conquered than evaded by the risen Lord. Furthermore, the automatic immortality which the Christian Scientists seem to proclaim is at variance with the solemn warning of Christ and his apostles that there is a way of salvation and a way of damnation.

One is bound to admire the consistent idealism, both philosophical and moral, in the teachings of Mrs Eddy, but her life was not always totally consistent with her teachings. She wore artificial teeth and spectacles, so that obviously her practice of Christian Science was not completely successful, but these facts do not invalidate the applicability of Christian Science teachings to illnesses of the teeth and eyes.

A more serious failure was publicly revealed in a protest addressed to the trustees of Mrs Eddy by Mr John V. Dittemore (a former director of the mother church of Christian Science) in the course of which he wrote: 'As you will know, Mrs Eddy employed physicians professionally, and took drugs on numerous occasions in the last ten years of her life.'[9] On the other hand, though it is rarely referred to by orthodox Christian Scientists, there is a passage in *Science and Health*[10] in which Mrs Eddy recommends Christian Scientists to seek the services of a surgeon for broken or dislocated bones.

Mrs Eddy's philosophy of life deviates in two important respects from historic Christian doctrine: namely, in her teaching about the personality of God and the nature and work of Jesus Christ.

Her views of God seem to oscillate between the impersonal and the sentimental. An example of the impersonal reference to God is the following: 'Life, truth, and love constitute the triune Person called God, that is, the triply Divine principle, Love.'[11] A principle is so much less than a person. Furthermore, her teaching represents a serious deviation from the Christian doctrine of the Holy Trinity, as the following statement makes evident: 'Jesus demonstrated Christ; he proved that Christ is the divine idea of God – the Holy Ghost, or Comforter, revealing the Divine principle, Love.'[12] An impersonal principle with such personal attributes as love is an impossibility. The sentimental reference, in which anthropomorphism runs riot, is found in the references to 'Father-Mother God'.[13]

Hers is also a heretical account of the person of Jesus Christ. In fact, it is a combination of two heresies. At times it can be accused of Docetism in denying the reality of Christ's human nature. She writes:

> Wearing in part a human form (that is, as it seemed to mortal view), being conceived by a human mother, Jesus was a Mediator between Spirit and the flesh, between Truth and error.[14]

The other heresy of which her christology is guilty is that of Nestorianism. In her view 'Jesus' referred to the human and 'Christ' to the divine natures of the God-man. They are always sharply distinguished and there is no communication of the power of one nature to the other in the personhood of Christ. Thus when she refers to 'Jesus' or to 'Christ', she does not intend her words to refer to the other nature, and the result is inevitably dichotomous.

The major treatment of the person of Jesus Christ reads, in excerpted form, as follows:

> Jesus was born of Mary. Christ is the true idea voicing good, the divine message from God to men speaking to the human consciousness ... The corporeal man Jesus was human ... Jesus demonstrated Christ; he proved that Christ is the divine idea of God – the Holy Ghost, or Comforter, revealing the divine Principle, Love, and leading into all truth. Jesus was the Son of a virgin ... The word *Christ* is not properly a synonym for Jesus, though it is commonly so used ... The divine image, idea, or Christ was, is, and ever will be inseparable from the divine Principle, God ... By these sayings Jesus meant, not that the

human Jesus was or is eternal, but that the divine idea or Christ was and is so and therefore antedated Abraham.[15]

It is clear from this passage that the Christ is an eternal idea and Jesus merely its temporal and temporary form, and that only the idea of the Logos has eternity, whereas the orthodox christology of Chalcedon excluded these very views when put forward by Nestorius as heretical. In partial exculpation, however, it could with truth be said that this was the most Christian of the heresies condemned by that Council, and that a Nestorian church came into being which has outlived persecution and survived vigorously to our own day!

The Docetism is apparent in unmistakable fashion in the denial that Jesus actually died on the cross. In her other volume, *Miscellany*, Mrs Eddy speaks of 'the supposedly crucified Jesus' and interprets St Paul's statement in Romans 5.10 as meaning 'for when we were enemies, we were reconciled to God, by the seeming death of his Son'. At one point she even claims to have understood the Christ-event better than the apostles in the astonishing statement:

> Jesus' students, not sufficiently advanced fully to understand their Master's triumph, did not perform many wonderful works until they saw him after his crucifixion, and learned that he had not died.[16]

On the other hand, Mrs Eddy has a clear sense that if Christ did not die, he did overcome death in triumph. She wrote: 'The lonely precincts of the tomb gave Jesus a refuge from his foes, a place in which to solve the great problem of being. His three days' work in the sepulchre set the seal of eternity on time.'[17] This is hardly the Christian doctrine of Resurrection, since there must be a death before there is a resurrection; but it is an affirmation of immortality for Christ.

A denial of the doctrine of the Holy Trinity, and a denial of the reality of the Incarnation, the Cross and the Resurrection of Jesus Christ, raises serious doubts about the appropriateness of the term *Christian* in the title of her movement, Christian Science.

III

Apart from these distortions or denials of the historic Christian message, Christian Science must be accounted dangerous for other reasons. Many lives have been lost through the inability of Mrs Eddy and her Christian Scientist practitioners to distinguish between illness caused by germ invasion and illness caused by psychological factors. H. A. L. Fisher avers in *Our New Religion* that the refusal of Christian Scientists to collaborate with members of the medical profession lays them open to the charge of being murderers. While that may be an overstatement, one could at least argue with some probability of truth that they are parasites to the degree that they live on the precautions of preventive medicine and public health. Furthermore, it is significant that although Christian Science has great sums of money at its disposal, opulent premises and enthusiastic workers, it is rarely found bringing its mission of health and happiness where it is most needed – in the slums.

The Christian Scientists appear to have little interest in the social implications of the Christian gospel. They show little concern for lessening inter-ethnic tensions, in building orphanages or old-age homes for the poor, or in supporting institutions in higher education except those that teach their own particular tenets.

They can be accused of making religion a means to an end: God is the means and the end is man's physical well-being. This, however, is a travesty of Mrs Eddy's own intention. 'Healing physical sickness,' she wrote, 'is the smallest part of Christian Science. It is only the bugle-call in thought and action, in the higher range of infinite goodness. The emphatic purpose of Christian Science is the healing of sin; and this task may be harder than the cure of disease; because while mortals love to sin, they do not love to be sick.'[18] On that shrewd and eminently balanced judgment, we leave the exposition of the thought of Mary Baker Eddy.

IV

We have noticed a certain theological or metaphysical escapism in the idealistic thought of Mary Baker Eddy, reminiscent of the fable of the three Indian monkeys who are determined to occlude evil. At the same time it would have to be conceded that Christian Science is no system to attract the indolent or the undisciplined. On the contrary, Christian Science has a rigorous discipline of its own. It forbids alcohol, tobacco or drugs and requires daily reading of both the Bible and *Science and Health*. Christian Science is a spiritual ally in an increasingly materialist world, but it has decidedly determined on its own authoritative interpretation of the

Christian revelation in *Science and Health*, which is read immediately after each biblical lesson in its services. that it is difficult to see possibilities of either ecumenical rapprochement or of *aggorniamento* bringing it closer to the historic Christian churches in the near future. That is a pity. Not only because members of the Christian family should live harmoniously, but because the historic churches need to recover the sense of the Christian contribution to health and the leadership that women can bring to Christian organization. These gifts Christian Science is peculiarly equipped by its history and its emphasis to give, and for its escapist tendency (both philosophically and socially) it requires the realism and universalism of the historic churches.

NOTES

1. E. S. Bates and J. W. Dittemore, *The Truth and the Tradition*, Knopf, New York 1932. See also Horatio Dresser, *The Quimby Manuscripts,* Crowell, New York 1921.

2. Mary Baker Eddy, *Science and Health*, Christian Science Publishing Co., Boston, Mass., p.110.

3. Christian Science publishes no official statistics. See the basis on which this estimate is made in Charles S. Braden, *Christian Science Today*, Southern Methodist University Press, Dallas, Texas 1958, p.272.

4. *Science and Health*, p.468.

5. Ibid., p.113.

6. Ibid., p.460.

7. Ibid., p.413.

8. Ibid., pp.413f.

9. Reported in *The Christian World* (of London), 28 February 1929, and cited in Leslie D. Weatherhead, *Psychology in the Service of the Soul*, Epworth Press, London 1949, p.219.

10. See p.401 in Science and Health. My attention has been drawn to this by Mr David McIlhiney, friend and doctoral candidate in religion at Princeton University.

11. *Science and Health*, p.331.

12. Ibid., p.332.

13. Ibid., p.332.

14. Ibid., p.315.

15. Ibid., pp.332-4.

16. Ibid., p.45.

17. Ibid., p.44.

18. *Rudimental Divine Science,* Christian Science Publishing Co., Boston, Mass., p.2.

FURTHER READING

Eddy, Mary Baker: her own writings are the basic sources for the study of Christian Science, and the chief of them, all published by the Christian

Science Publishing Co., Boston, Mass., are: *Science and Health, with Key to the Scriptures* and *Miscellaneous Writings*.

Beasley, Norman, *The Cross and the Crown; the History of Christian Science*, New York 1952.

Braden, C. S., *Christian Science Today*, Southern Methodist University Press, Dallas 1958.

Fisher, H. A. L., *Our New Religion*, Watts, London 1929, severely critical of the movement.

Peel, Robert, *Christian Science. Its Encounter with American Culture*, Henry Holt and Co., New York 1958.

Peel, Robert, *Mary Baker Eddy: The Years of Discovery 1821-1875*, Holt, Rinehart and Winston, New York 1966.

Peel, Robert, *Mary Baker Eddy*, vol. 2, Holt, Rinehart and Winston, New York 1971.

Wilbur, Sibyl, *The Life of Mary Baker Eddy*, Christian Science Publishing Co., Boston, Mass. 1938 — the official life.

5 The Mormons

*For other foundation can no man lay
than that which is laid, which is Jesus
Christ* (I Corinthians 3.11)

The 'Church of Jesus Christ of Latter-Day Saints' is the official
title by which the Mormons are known. The briefer description
is derived from the *Book of Mormon*, which forms a part of
their supplements to the Holy Scriptures of the Old and New
Testaments. They began as a nineteenth-century American
religious movement on the moving westward frontier, who
succeeded in the teeth of many hazards in establishing a theo-
cratic community in Utah. This God-ruled community resembled
in many ways the ideals of the godly Puritans of New England
in the seventeenth century, especially in its affirmation of obedience to the purpose of God, its ethical rigour and discipline, the
high priority it gave to education and its sense of being the
church of the elect (with the corollary that other churches were
apostates of one kind or another). There is a striking parallel
in nomenclature, too. The Puritan Independents called themselves 'Visible Saints'; the Mormons call themselves 'Latter-Day
Saints'.

What factors help to account for the spread of the Mormon
faith?

To begin with, this is a religious movement with an outstand-
ing history of courage. No one can read the story of the 'Great
Trek' westward from Nauvoo to the Great Salt Lake without
admiration for the heroism of the pioneers. Thomas O'Dea
describes its start in these words:

The Mormons began their exodus on the morning of February 4, 1846. Before Dawn, ferries started taking the shivering
evacuees across the ice-choked Mississippi. The temperature

was twenty below zero and the wind bitter. In the freezing camp of their first night on the road nine babies were born. At eleven o'clock on the morning of February 15, Brigham Young crossed the river with a party and followed the first two thousand pilgrims to Sugar Creek, nine miles beyond, where a temporary rude shelter was set up. The great Mormon trek had begun under the most inauspicious circumstances. On the first month on the road they never made more than six miles a day.[1]

A Catholic priest, Father De Smet, estimated that by the fall of 1846 the number of persons at Council Bluffs was 10,000; others put the figure at 15,000. On 24 July 1847 many reached the Salt Lake Valley, and this day is kept as Pioneer Day in Utah. This great movement from persecution and aided by faith was under the superb leadership of Brigham Young. It is most moving to think of the elderly as well as the women and children who engaged in the hazardous enterprise, especially as one revisualizes them in the sculptures in the central square of Salt Lake City today, observing the handcarts that the poorest pushed with their pitiable bundle of possessions. This is a saga of intrepid heroism and invincible spirit, and the retelling of it has won friends for the Mormons.

A second impressive factor is the militant missionary spirit of Mormonism. Who cannot fail to be impressed by the zeal that sends so many healthy, mature and strong-minded young missionaries to lands overseas to witness for the Church of Jesus Christ of Latter-Day Saints? For the two (sometimes four) years they are on missionary duty the young Mormons so designated have to support themselves and to pay their own travel costs. Such independence, integrity of character and altruism are bound to make an impact on unprejudiced observers.

A third factor accounting for the attraction to Mormonism is the remarkable reputation of the state of Utah, in which the Mormons are in the great majority. It has a nationwide reputation for excellence in public education (from kindergarten to university levels), and it is said that a higher percentage of the population of Utah goes to college and gains PhD degrees than is the case in any other state in the Union. It is also renowned for health and public welfare. Its citizens are justly respected for their industry, sobriety, frugality, temperance and honesty – those Puritan virtues which have become much rarer in our own day.

In the fourth place, the Mormons, like the Roman Catholics, are reputed to know how to look after their own members of the faithful. Their strong community spirit is very supportive of the poor, the weak and the aged. In Vermont, for example, from which their founder Joseph Smith hailed, it is their effective help to poor but industrious farmers by lending them capital and making it possible for them to hire modern agricultural machinery that has caused several families to join the Mormons. Who can blame them?

Fifthly, the Mormons claim through Joseph Smith to have received a revelation of God for America, and that their sacred books prove it. This was clearly a telling point for Americans, though it could be a missionary disadvantage outside the States for those who are not impressed by manifest American destiny. Furthermore, this American type of theology is attractive to many because it takes a more optimistic view of human nature than orthodox Christianity with its doctrine of the Fall and original sin, for it denies original sin, and it also asserts that no soul can ever be destroyed. Furthermore, it stresses man's active co-operation with God.

In the sixth place, the generosity of Mormons in contributing to their faith is proverbial. They do not only give a tenth of their income to the church, but they also have 'fast offerings' on the first Sunday of each month when they donate the monetary equivalent of the two meals they have gone without for the support of the poor.

One might further add that if their history of polygamy in the nineteenth century hung like an albatross around their necks, the pre-eminence of two twentieth-century Mormons as members of the Cabinet (President Eisenhower's Secretary of Agriculture was Ezra Taft Benson, and George Romney, former Governor of Michigan, is a member of President Nixon's Cabinet) has shown the average American a glimpse of the qualities of leadership and business acumen among the leading Mormons.

I

The history of Mormonism is the key with which to unlock its beliefs, practices and spirit.

Its founder, Joseph Smith, was born in the village of Sharon in the State of Vermont in 1805. In those days and in that area the opportunity for education was slight, but they specialized in the making of character. Smith described himself as 'a rough stone, desiring the learning of heaven alone'. At the age of fifteen, he claimed to have seen a vision and received a call to become 'a prophet of the Most High God'. In 1823 he further claimed to have received an angelic messenger who came to him directly from the divine presence. The burden of the message was that Smith would find a precious religious volume hidden in a hill. He was also told that this volume was written on plates of gold and contained the history of the former inhabitants of the North American continent as well as the fullest account of the gospel as delivered by Christ to the ancient inhabitants. He was also instructed that, with the divine assistance and the aid of two crystals, he would be able to interpret this volume.

Four years later he claimed that the angel of God instructed him where to look for the golden volume and that he immediately dug it up. He maintained that these golden plates were inscribed in writing that the Mormons have later identified as 'Reformed Egyptian'. With the aid of the promised crystals, and the assistance of God, he claimed he was enabled to translate the script. This translation was not done word for word, but passage by passage. Mormons today affirm that it was given in King James English to make it readily intelligible to Smith's associates. This is the not altogether convincing explanation they give to account for the use of 27,000 words of the King James or Authorized Version of the scriptures, and for the rather unusual fact that the translation has references to Christ before his nativity and uses such words as 'Bible'. It seems more than strange that a relatively unlettered but otherwise able man was able to translate 'Reformed Egyptian' years before the oriental scholars of the world were able to decipher Egyptian inscriptions with the discovery of the Rosetta stone. We must choose between a great miracle and a great illusion for the explanation of these events; but if ethical fruits are any test, then the miraculous explanation is perhaps to be preferred.

The *Book of Mormon*, for such it was that Smith claimed to have found in the hill, purports to describe the inhabitants of the Western hemisphere during the years from 600 BC to AD 400. It is made up of fourteen books and an editorial note. The first theme of the book is the arrival and settlement of Hebrews on the continent of America before the Christian era, and this is introduced to explain the origin of the American Indians. America is seen as the land of promise, and there is the strong message that virtue and prosperity begin a cycle that leads to pride and inequity, social divisions and arrogance, to sin and decadence, and from there to the chastisement of the Lord. If this does not end in destruction, it is followed by repentance and the reinstatement of rights, and the theme has come full cycle.

It is worth drawing attention to the romantic nationalism of the book, for a prophet calls this 'a land which is choice above all other lands' (II Nephi 1.5) and the sanctification of immigration to America appears in the next verse, where it is said that 'there shall none come into this land save that they shall be brought by the hand of the Lord'.

A summary of the contents of the *Book of Mormon* is best given in Smith's own words:

> We are informed by these records that America in ancient times has been inhabited by two distinct races of people. The first were called Jaredites, and came directly from the Tower of Babel. The second race came directly from the city of Jerusalem about six hundred years before Christ. They were principally Israelites, of the descendants of Joseph. The Jaredites were destroyed about the time that the Israelites came from Jerusalem, who succeeded them in the inhabitance of the country. The principal nation of the second race fell in battle towards the end of the fourth century. The remnant are the *Indians* who now inhabit the country. The book also tells us that our Saviour also made his appearance upon this continent after his Resurrection: that he planted the gospel here in all its fulness and richness, and power and blessing; that they had apostles, prophets, pastors, teachers, evangelists; the same order, the same priesthood, the same ordinances, gifts, powers and blessing as was enjoyed on the Eastern Continent; that the people were cut off in consequence of their transgressions; that the last of their prophets who existed among them was commanded to write an abridgement of their prophecies, history, etc. and to hide it up in the earth, and that it should come forth and be united with the Bible for the accomplishment of the purpose of God in the last days.[2]

From being a passive translator, Smith developed into being a prophet and legislator with the publication of the *Book of Doctrine and Covenants*. These combined an insistence upon the imminence of the Second Advent with a demand to revive the charismatic signs of the primitive church, including miracles, the gift of tongues, faith-healing, prophecies and – most important of all – continued revelations. The latter principle gave Joseph Smith the flexibility he needed to interpret the will of God in new situations, but it also virtually ended the view that the revelation of Jesus Christ as recorded in the scriptures had finality. This was, inevitably, the principle that encouraged deviations from historic Christianity.

The new religious community became increasingly unpopular amongst its neighbours because of the conviction that God was commanding them to practise plural marriage, or polygamy, as was the case with the Old Testament patriarchs. In consequence, it became necessary to move away. The next kingdom of the elect of God was to be in Missouri. Thence, after further strenuous objections on the part of their neighbours, the Mormons moved on to the vicinity of Commerce in Illinois. There they founded the town of Nauvoo. Here, again, they faced further persecution. At the request of the governor of the state, Joseph Smith and his brother Hyrum were imprisoned in Carthage. On 27 June 1844, a mob with faces blackened to prevent their recognition broke into the prison and shot the two brothers. The effect of this dastardly act was to transform Joseph Smith from a gifted leader into a martyr and a legend.

The prophet's mantle fell upon the ample shoulders of Brigham Young, who wore it for a further thirty years and was the second father of his people. He it was who led a large party into the promised land of Utah. He formulated the policy that the Indians on their borders should be fed rather than fought. He organized the chief settlements and the pioneering ways of immigration and irrigation. He was appointed as governor of the territory of Utah. For thirty hard years he presided over the church that Joseph Smith had founded, and was a veritable patriarch to all his people. He inspired the building of temples, tabernacles and theatres. He founded schools and organized a newspaper. He headed the great mercantile and industrial movements in his area until his death in 1877. A great city – Salt Lake, and a great State – Utah, are his living memorial, as well as being an abiding monument to Mormon faith and industry.

The last great problem the Mormons faced in the nineteenth century was polygamy. Joseph Smith and his associates had practised plural marriage, even though they had lived in the strictly monogamous traditions of New England prior to their westward move. (A wit had declared, with more humour than truth, that the Mormons left Nauvoo 'with their creed singular and their wives plural'.) In 1862 Congress passed a law prohibiting polygamy.

which was reinforced and strengthened twenty years later. The Mormons did not readily give up their polygamy, partly because they believed they had a 'revelation' from Smith, and presumably partly also for obvious demographic reasons – to build up the holy community by natural augmentation. But they increasingly fell foul of the laws in Utah, Idaho and Arizona, which were vigorously prosecuted against them. As a result, Mormon leaders were driven into exile, and many men and women were imprisoned and more fined. In 1890 President Woodruff, the Mormon leader, offered the United States Government a manifesto, submitting himself to the anti-polygamous laws and promising to try and persuade the members of the church to follow his example. This caused great unhappiness in many Mormon families, because it meant that compliance with the laws required a husband to put away all wives except the first, and many of them were greatly beloved. Not only that, but it virtually rendered all children of the second and subsequent wives illegitimate. Many Mormons continued to support their large families though they could legally have deserted them. Gradually the Mormon community became monogamous, and in 1896 Utah was admitted into the Union.

II

What are the primary tenets of Mormon belief and practice? While there are many doctrines which resemble Protestant teaching (e.g. faith in Jesus Christ, repentance, and baptism for the remission of sins, atonement for all through the sacrifice of Christ), there are many distinctive teachings of the Church of Jesus Christ of Latter-Day Saints.

One novelty is the belief that there are two sources of doctrine: the written word of God, the scriptures, and direct revelation from God through continuous revelation. The former source includes the Bible, as far as this is translated correctly. To this is added the *Book of Mormon* translated by Joseph Smith; *Doctrine and Covenants*, a collection of revelations given chiefly through Smith; *The Pearl of Great Price*, containing revelations and writings of Abraham and Moses not found in the Bible. Continuous revelation comes directly from God (as to Moses in Exodus 33.11), or through the visitations of angels (as to Zacharias in Luke 1.11-20), or by impressions on man's mind made by the Spirit (as suggested in Ezekiel 11.5). The source of continuing revelation is the president of the church, and his official word, when speaking in the name of the

Lord, is received by the church as the word of God. Without question, this view of both supplementary scripture and continuing revelation removes the finality of Christ's revelation for this world. This is why it is unacceptable to the historic Christian churches.

Another distinctive doctrine of the Latter-Day Saints is their interpretation of the Trinity, which becomes tritheistic. God the Father has primary authority, Jesus Christ secondary authority, and the Spirit even less authority. Jesus Christ is believed to be literally the only-begotten Son of God in the flesh, and not to have been conceived as the other churches have affirmed – by the Holy Ghost. It is also believed that there are other gods for other planets, and that the God of this earth is in a state of progression, and that men may become gods.

The Mormons have an optimistic view of the nature of man, utterly denying the doctrines of the Fall and original sin. They believe that happiness is the normal expectancy of life: 'Men are, that they might have joy' (*Book of Mormon*: II Nephi, 2.25). Man, according to Mormon belief, was in the beginning with God, that is, he has gone through a long pre-mortal existence (*Doctrine and Covenants*, 93.23). After he dies and is resurrected, he will receive an immortal body. Moreover, the Mormons are universalists, believing that all men will be resurrected through the atonement of Jesus Christ. But there are degrees of glory and estate in eternal life. Heaven is envisaged as offering eternal life and eternal progress in the company of one's loved ones.

The Mormons also believe that they are the only true church, and that all the other churches are in varying degrees of apostasy. To unchurch all other Christians seems uncharitable in the extreme, unless we assert the belief that all will eventually be won to Christ. Joseph Smith's tolerant view of other religions may be judged from the following citation taken from *Times and Seasons* (15 April 1842):

The great designs of God in relation to the salvation of the human family are very little understood by the professedly wise and intelligent generation in which we live ... The Mussulman condemns the heathen, the Jew, and the Christian and the whole world of mankind that reject his Koran, as infidels, and consigns the whole of them to perdition. The Jew believes that the whole world that rejects his faith and are not circumcised are Gentile dogs, and will be damned. The heathen is equally as tenacious about his principles, and the Christian consigns all to perdition who cannot bow to his creed, and submit to his *ipse dixit*.

But while one portion of the human race is judging and condemning the other without mercy. the Great Parent of the universe looks upon the whole of the human family with a fatherly care and paternal regard; He views them as his offspring, and without any of those contracted feelings that influence the children of men, causes 'his sun to rise on the evil and the good, and sendeth rain on the just and the unjust'... He will judge them not according to what they have not, but according to what they have. Those who have lived without law will be judged without law, and those who have a law, will be judged by that law.

Sometimes Mormons have been accused of having a Smithocentric rather than a Christocentric faith, but this is a serious misrepresentation of their view. Christ is not regarded as an ordinary or even extraordinary mortal. He is unique as the only-begotten Son of the Father. Joseph Smith is thought of as a great religious leader, like Moses, or as a great prophet, like Isaiah or Ezekiel. His prime importance among the prophets derives from the Mormon conviction that he is the great prophet of this dispensation of the true gospel.

Mormons do not believe that there has been a final revelation of Christ, nor will there be until the second coming of Christ in glory; at that time revelation will no longer be necessary because Christ will reign personally on the earth. Until that time arises, however, the guidance of Christ through revelation given to his servants, the successive presidents of the Church of Jesus Christ of Latter-Day Saints, is necessary to prevent the true doctrines of Christ being perverted by the doctrines of men. If an orthodox Christian were to challenge this viewpoint by insisting that Christ is the final revelation of God, the astute Mormon would reply that corrupt teachings have been added to the Bible and in any case it was not complete, hence the necessity for the supplemental scriptures like the *Book of Mormon*. This, then, like the Mormon doctrine of the Trinity, which is a tritheistic subordinationism is a deviation from Christian orthodoxy.

The Mormons have two distinctive customs of great interest. One is known as 'baptism for the dead' and the second is called 'celestial marriage'. The former is a vicarious baptism undertaken by living Mormons for their dead ancestors who might otherwise miss the joys of heaven, or suffer delay in attaining to them. This custom has been acutely described as a 'retro-active application of the Roman Catholic doctrine of purgatory'.[3] Apart from ordinary marriage vows which last until death, the Mormons encourage 'celestial marriage' which lasts beyond death. It is an exceedingly romantic notion and indicates the great mutual affection between Mormon husbands and wives. For the orthodox Christian, however, it is an unacceptable practice, because Christ taught that in heaven there is neither marriage nor giving in marriage.

The ethics of Mormonism are simple, yet demanding, as may be seen from the following citations:

> That inasmuch as any man drinketh wine or strong drink among you, behold it is not good, neither meet in the sight of your Father...
>
> And, again, strong drinks are not for the body, neither for the belly, but for the washing of your bodies.
>
> And, again, tobacco is not for the body, neither for the belly, and is not good for man, but is an herb for bruises and all sick cattle, to be used with judgment and skill.
>
> And, again, hot drinks are not for the body or belly.[4]

However much the orthodox Christian may admire the courage, the faith, the social and educational concern and the missionary zeal of the Church of Jesus Christ of Latter-Day Saints, there remain certain difficulties for him. Some we have already touched upon: a progressive revelation which supplements and revises parts of the New Testament, the idea of a progressive God conceived as an artificer, tritheism instead of the Holy Trinity, and the custom of 'celestial marriage'. But these do not exhaust the problems.

The *Book of Mormon* raises difficulties because of its cultural and theological anachronisms. Laban is given a steel sword in 600 BC (I Nephi 4.9); horses, cows, oxen and asses are discovered in the New World (I Nephi 18.25). Even though the Mosaic Law prohibits it, the Jaredites use swine (Ether 9.18). Even less plausible is the references of prophets and seers to 'Jesus Christ', 'the Son of God', and to his death and resurrection. Furthermore, the Christian doctrines of the atonement in Christ, Christ's resurrection and baptism seem to be common articles of belief on the part of the Nephite prophets and their charges. Thomas O'Dea rightly says: 'It is as if the author could not imagine Hebraic Messianic hopes in any other terms than Christian.'[5]

There are also great difficulties in the authority of the *Book of Mormon*, unless one is a Mormon. We know of no other writings produced in 'Reformed Egyptian'. Do we know of any pre-Columbian gold plates with the writings of early Americans? Until we receive convincing answers to such questions, it would only be unreasonable not to employ Occam's razor.

Before leaving the Mormons, it should be mentioned that there is another group known as the Reorganized Church of Jesus Christ of Latter-Day Saints. This church claims to be the legal successor of the Church of Latter-Day Saints founded by Joseph Smith at Fayette, New York, in 1830. After the death of Joseph Smith in 1844, the original church is said to have broken up into factions following various leaders. This group rejected the leadership of Brigham Young who went with the great majority to Utah. Those who remained rejected polygamy, partly re-established themselves at Independence, Missouri, in 1862, as the 'Reorganized Church', and completed their organization in 1860 when Joseph Smith III, son of the founder, accepted leadership and was chosen president of the church, which he remained until his death in 1914. It is interesting that the 'Reorganized Church' stresses more strongly than its competitor the authority of the New Testament, and, in the use of ministers, seems closer to the Protestant churches.

The latter judgment raises the interesting question as to whether there are any prospects for dialogue between Mormons and the historic Christian churches. The prospects would be bleak if it were thought that a precondition were to be any compromises on doctrine, or if the ranks of the Mormons considered that there was a plot to get them to become part of the World Council of Churches. The reason for the suspicion of ecumenism is that this is thought to be a scheme to make a church in which everyone will be forced to believe the same things. But if the primary purpose of dialogue is to create a better understanding across the present divide, which if maintained, can only breed further suspicion and misunderstanding, then such a dialogue is highly desirable. For mutual respect is greatly to be desired among Protestants, Catholics and Mormons.

NOTES

1. Thomas O'Dea, *The Mormons*, University of Chicago Press, Chicago 1957, pp.76f.

2. Smith's article is printed in I. D. Rupp, *An Original History of the Denominations of the United States*, 1844, p.4.

3. 'Saints, Latter Day' – article by I. W. Riley in Hastings, *Encyclopaedia of Religion and Ethics*, Vol. XI.

4. *Doctrine and Covenants*, 89.5,7-9.

5. O'Dea, op. cit., p.39.

FURTHER READING

The chief original sources are: *Book of Mormon*, 1830; *Doctrine and Covenants*, 1833; and *The Pearl of Great Price*, 1851. Also important is *Brigham Young's Discourses*, ed. John A. Widstoe, Deseret Book Co., Salt Lake City, Utah 1925. The official history is Joseph Fielding Smith, *Documentary History of the Church*, 7 Vols., Deseret Press, Salt Lake City, Utah 1949, and the same writer has produced a doctrinal compendium entitled *The Doctrines of Salvation*, 3 vols., Bookcraft, Salt Lake City, Utah 1956. An older valuable book on doctrine is that of James E. Talmadge, *The Articles of Faith*. The Church of Jesus Christ of Latter-Day Saints, Salt Lake City 1924.

Other sympathetic accounts of great interest are:

Ericksen, Ephraim E., *The Psychological and Ethical Aspects of Mormonism*, University of Chicago Press 1911.

O'Dea, Thomas, *The Mormons,* University of Chicago Press 1957.

Whalen, William J., *The Latter-Day Saints in the Modern Day World*, John Day, New York 1964.

6 Jehovah's Witnesses

*But now abideth faith, hope and
charity; and the greatest of these is
charity* (I Corinthians 13.13)

Jehovah's Witnesses is the final name chosen by a sect which
has been known variously as 'The Millennial Dawn', 'The International Bible Students Association', 'The Watchtower Organization', and the company of those who subscribe to the doctrine
'Millions now living will never die!' The present designation of this
body was applied to it by 'Judge' Rutherford in 1931 and is based
upon the words of the prophet, 'Ye are my witnesses, saith Jehovah'.[1] This prolific group has come into the public eye by reason
of its pertinacious tract-sellers and because its adherents refuse to
accept military service or blood transfusion. In 1966 there were
24,158 congregations of Witnesses, of which 5,141 were to be found
in the United States. Their total membership throughout the world
(about 200 countries) was 1,109,806, of which 330,358 were in the
United States.

I

The sect originated in the mind of Charles Taze Russell at Alleg-
hany, Pittsburgh, in 1872. Then aged twenty, he was a member of
the local Congregational church and of the YMCA in the neigh-
bourhood. The real forerunners of the movement, however, were a
group of Second Adventists and, in particular, a J. H. Paton, to
whose writings Russell was greatly indebted, though it was beneath him to acknowledge this.

Russell was a wealthy haberdasher, who had inherited five
shops from his father, but sold them in order to devote his entire
working days to the dissemination of his views. As a speaker he

was compelling, and as an organizer efficient. In 1874 he founded a new religious organization named the Zion's Watch Tower Society. Apart from a magazine which he edited and largely wrote, and a mass of tracts which he composed, he produced a seven-volume series entitled *Studies in the Scriptures*, which is the main compendium of the doctrines of the Witnesses. The movement spread to England in 1880 and in a further eight years its representatives were active in China, India, Turkey, Haiti and Africa.

Russell is a curiously disreputable figure to have originated a new religious movement. So overweening was his egotism that he claimed to be a competent Greek scholar, though, as was proved in court, he hardly knew a letter of the alphabet of that language. His domineering conceit and wayward affections became widely known when his wife sued him for divorce and her petition was readily granted. He was accused by the *Brooklyn Eagle* of selling grain, which he advertised as 'miracle-wheat', at sixty dollars a bushel, and he admitted that there was 'some element of truth' in the charge. He was also believed to have played upon the fears of sick persons to induce them to make over their fortunes to his organization. This was all the more hypocritical of him as he jibed at the moneys collected by the Christian churches and advertised Witness gatherings as 'No Collection Meetings'. His egotism was boundless, for he stated in the introductory pages of his *Studies in the Scriptures* that it would be better to leave the Bible unopened and to read his commentary on it, than to omit the latter and read only the Bible.

Russell died in October 1916. So impressed was the attorney of the Witnesses, the misnamed 'Judge' Rutherford, that he wrote:

> When the history of the Church of Christ is fully written, it will be found that the place next to St Paul in the gallery of fame as expounders of the Gospel of the great Master will be occupied by Charles Taze Russell.[2]

It is hardly surprising that so ardent a devotee of the founder of the movement should have been elected to succeed him. From 1917 until his death in 1942, Rutherford led the Witnesses with an iron but successful hand. He, too, was a prolific writer and he implemented the propaganda of the organization by a radio network and the sale of gramophone records of his addresses. In 1942 Nathan Knorr succeeded Rutherford.

Despite its popularity, however, the movement was banned in several countries because its adherents refused the duties of citizenship and proselytized amongst the members of the Christian churches. They were proscribed in Northern Rhodesia, after a disturbance in the Copper Belt in the nineteen-thirties. In 1940 and 1941 the New Zealand and Australian governments outlawed them as a subversive organization. In January 1947 the Supreme Court of Canada ruled that they 'were not a religious body' and in the same year they were banned in Southern Rhodesia. About 6,000 of them suffered in Hitler's concentration camps.[3]

II

One of the main reasons for their success in terms of statistics is their autocratic and hierarchic type of organization. This is marked by all the efficiency characteristic of a modern international businesshouse. At the head is a central, all-powerful Board of Directors. Under this Board and responsible to it are the various 'Religious Servants' and beneath them the many 'Circuit Servants'. Below them are the 'District Servants', and the 'Branch Servants' below the latter. Local groups are known as 'Congregations', each of which meets in a 'Kingdom Hall' overseen by a 'Congregational Servant'. He is assisted by a 'service committee' which takes charge of various activities, particularly of the 'back calls', that is, repeated visiting of contacts. Women are discouraged from seeking office, and each member of the hierarchy obeys the orders of his superior without question.

The chief task of the Witnesses is the distribution of the official publications from door to door. Each member is expected to assume his share of these duties and many are equipped with a portable gramophone on which recordings of Rutherford's sermons are played to the householders. All details of visits have to be reported on specially printed forms to the Board of Directors at headquarters. In brief, the Witnesses are organized as a group of religious commercial travellers.

A survey of their teaching will reveal that the Jehovah's Witnesses are heretics, in addition to being schismatics. In their doctrine of God they are monotheistic, if not definitely unitarian. Perhaps their teaching about the person of Christ is most akin to the Arian heresy of the fourth century AD, for they assert that the Son of God is a created being. This is the purport of the following citation from Russell:

As he (Jesus) was the highest of all Jehovah's creation, so

also was he the first, the direct creation of God, the 'only Begotten', and then he, as Jehovah's power, and in his name, created all things...[4]

Russell repudiates the Chalcedonian Definition's claim that in Jesus Christ the divine and human natures co-existed:

Neither was Jesus a combination of the two natures, human and spiritual. The blending of two natures produces neither the one nor the other, but an imperfect, hybrid thing, which is obnoxious to the divine arrangement.[5]

The Witnesses are committed to the curious belief that before his incarnation Jesus was the Archangel Michael, which they believe is taught in Dan. 12.1. They also hold that Jesus gave up his angelic nature in the days of his flesh and was an ordinary fallible mortal. They claim that, although Jesus was not divine, he paid at his death the ransom necessary to set men free from death, but that his work of atonement 'will be completed with the close of the Millennial Age'.[6] They further reduce the stature of the eternal Son of God by declaring that elect Christians, 'the little flock', will 'be reckoned as joint sacrificers, joint mediators, joint reconcilers' with Jesus.[7] Salvation largely consists in being imitators of Jesus, which argues, of course, self-salvation.

The Witnesses do not believe that the redeeming work of Christ was completed on the Cross or that those who have faith in him are saved from their sins and inherit eternal life. Russell taught:

The 'ransom for all' given by 'the man Christ Jesus' does not give or guarantee everlasting life or blessing to any man; but it does guarantee to every man another opportunity or trial for life everlasting.[8]

Thus, far from being saved by Christ, each man must work out his own salvation:

Some have been blinded in part, and some completely, by the God of this world, and they must be recovered from blindness as well as from death, that they, *each for himself*, may have a full chance to prove, by obedience or disobedience, their worthiness or unworthiness of life eternal.[9]

This is clearly justification by works, not justification by faith.

The Witnesses also believe that Jesus was provided with a new spiritual body at the resurrection, and that his human body was neither raised nor glorified. In one place Russell teaches:

> He was put to death *a man*, but was raised from the dead a *spirit being* of the highest order of the divine nature...[10]

In another he declares:

> Our Lord's human body was, however, supernaturally removed from the tomb; because had it remained there it would have been an insurmountable obstacle to the faith of the disciples, who were not yet instructed in spiritual things...[11]

Significantly (for the Witnesses are essentially a commercial organization), the permanent status of the Ascended Christ is described as being 'the Chief Executive Officer of Jehovah'.[12]

It is not surprising that the Witnesses find the doctrine of the Trinity irrational, since they have reduced the status of the eternal Son of God to that of a fallible mortal and conceive of the Holy Spirit as merely the invisible influence of Jehovah.[13]

They have a ghoulish fondness for the text, 'The wages of sin is death.' They claim that all men are destroyed in death, but that all the dead will be raised again and given a second chance at the Second Advent of Christ. In making such assertions they ignore the promise made by our Lord to the penitent thief, 'This day thou shalt be with me in Paradise', and the implications of the metaphor by which the New Testament describes the dead as those 'that are fallen asleep in Christ'. The doctrine of the second chance is an encouragement to libertarians, apart from its infidelity to the New Testament insistence on the way of salvation and the way of damnation as irrevocable destinies of men. This doctrine alone gives substance to the taunt that the teaching of the Jehovah's Witnesses is the religion of the natural man. Should evil men refuse the proffered salvation the second time, their fate will be annihilation, not eternal torment or damnation.

Despite the erroneous nature of much of this teaching the Witnesses can be congratulated on refusing to picture God as a divine sadist, whose dignity is established by the torturing of the damned. Rutherford taught:

> Eternal torture is void of the principle of love, 'God is love'. A Creator that would torture His creatures eternally would be a fiend, and not a God of love.[14]

Furthermore, the Witnesses teach that even death may be spiritually remedial. Their weakness is that they cannot conceive of divine love as *holy* love also: a world without rewards and punishments here and hereafter would be an immoral universe.

The unscriptural speculation of the Witnesses is given full scope in their account of the Second Advent and the millennium. Russell declared that the Seventh Millennium was the beginning of the reign of Christ. and he calculated that 1872 was the exact six-thousandth year from the creation of Adam and Eve. He prophesied that the final end of the world would take place in 1914. Since that time his followers have postponed the date to some time before 1984, when Gabriel's trumpet will blow and Christ will announce that the final end has come. Then God's 'Great Theocracy' will be established on earth, and Jehovah's Witnesses will be the only survivors to share in this divine kingdom.

Their account of the millennium is far more detailed than that offered by the Book of Revelation and they have already decided how the problem of feeding the resurrected bodies may be solved:

> Remembering the Lord's promise that in the Millennial period 'the earth shall yield her increase' and that the desert and the wilderness-places of the earth shall become as a Garden of Eden. we may safely estimate upon all the land, which we may find, according to recent estimates, to be 57,000,000 square miles or over 36,000,000,000 acres. What would this mean as to space for each person who has ever lived in the world, i.e. 28,441,126,838 persons? It means that there would be twelve-hundred and seventy-five acres for each little village of two hundred families. Quite a sufficiency of room, all will agree, under the new conditions promised. But if more space be necessary, with faith we will readily see that it will be quite within the divine power to raise vast continents from the depths of the ocean, or indeed to give a literal as well as a symbolical fulfilment to the declaration—'There shall be no more sea.'[15]

The only fitting retort to such speculations is that of Dr Reinhold Niebuhr, that faith has nothing to do with either the furniture of heaven or the temperature of hell!

After the battle of Armageddon the 144,000 faithful Jehovah's Witnesses will be taken up into heaven, there to rule with Christ over the new earth, which will be inhabited by the Jonadabs, or people of good will.

In our account of the beliefs of the Witnesses we cannot omit their loveless condemnation of the Christian churches as devil-controlled. There could be no worse offence against Christian charity than this typical citation from their teaching:

> These facts are set forth here, not for the purpose of holding men up to ridicule, but for the purpose of informing the people that the ecclesiastical systems, Catholic and Protestant, are under supervision and control of the Devil, and form a part of his visible organization, and therefore constitute the anti-Christ.[16]

A group claiming to be Christian, yet so vicious in its attitude to others who take the name of Christ on their lips, is guilty of an inner contradiction, for its spirit denies its profession.

In general, Jehovah's Witnesses fall under censure on four main characteristics. First, their doctrine is based upon an arbitrary selection of texts from the scriptures, but the main body of the teaching of Jesus and his apostles is either evaded or perverted; and to each ounce of the Bible a hundredweight of speculation is added.

In the second place, their doctrine is largely based upon the obscurities of such apocalyptic books as Daniel and Revelation, implying that the revelation of God is a tangled skein only to be unravelled by the subtle minds of this sect. But Christianity is not a mystery religion for initiates, for we 'have seen the glory of God in the face of Jesus Christ', who declared 'I am the light of the world'.

Thirdly, the use of the Bible as an *Old Moore's Almanac* of prediction is to misunderstand its purpose and to claim to know more than Jesus himself who confessed that he did not know the time of the coming of the Son of Man again on the clouds.

Fourthly, their creed must be rejected because it offers salvation on too easy terms, affirming, in effect, that payment for it may be deferred to another existence. This is to repudiate the solemn and urgent either-or of the Bible, and to sentimentalize the conception of a holy God. Moreover, as we have seen, this is a salvation by good works, not by faith in the victory of Christ. This is proven by the fact that only the worthy few are admitted to the single annual celebration of the Lord's Supper to receive the elements. In 1951, for instance, 623,760 Witnesses attended, but only 21,619 partook of the Supper.[17]

III

One further question remains to be answered: How have the devotees of such an unbalanced creed succeeded in winning so many members? This question is merely another way of asking: what can the churches learn from the strategy of Jehovah's Witnesses?

Russell's success was partly due to his clarity of thought, simplicity of expression in untechnical language and abundance of illustrations drawn from everyday life. Further, he and his followers have an unrivalled knowledge of Holy Writ and can quote chapter and verse for their opinions. It has been established that there are over 5,000 different scriptural citations in the books of Russell.[18] Jehovah's Witnesses have had the wisdom to assume and count upon every member being a propagandist of its organization, using the most up-to-date methods, such as gramophones, radios and attractively printed, bound and illustrated volumes.

Even their doctrines, in at least two cases, represent a healthy protest and reaction against current Christian orthodoxy. In their teaching about the 'last things' they refuse to accept the 'fire and brimstone' picture of hell and rightly protest against a doctrine that envisages punishment as vindictive, not remedial. The Jehovah's Witnesses, although denying the responsibilities of citizenship in so many ways, have protested against the devilries of modern warfare and the extravagance of modern life. It is also on record that their egalitarian convictions impelled them to welcome socialism even in its early days, when few religious folk were socialists. These, even when we condemn the Jehovah's Witnesses in so much, must be counted as its assets.

Their strongest asset, however, is the capacity for sacrifice. H. H. Stroup, an objective observer, says of them: 'They are willing to give up friends and family, to work indefatigably, to give unstintingly, to withstand bitter persecution, and even, in certain European countries, to remain loyal to their convictions unto death...'[19]

NOTES

1. Isa. 43.10.
2. Cited by H. H. Stroup, *The Jehovah's Witnesses*, Columbia University Press 1945, pp.12f.
3. Royston Pike, *Jehovah's Witnesses*, Watts, London, and Philosophical Library, New York 1954, p.26.

4. Charles Taze Russell, *Studies in the Scriptures*, V, p.84.

5. Ibid., I, p.179.

6. J. K. van Baalen, *The Chaos of Cults*, Eerdmans, Grand Rapids, Michigan 1938, p.147. See also Pike, op. cit., p.37.

7. Ibid.

8. *Studies in the Scriptures*, I, p.150.

9. Ibid., I, p.158.

10. Ibid., V, p.453.

11. Ibid., II, p.129.

12. Ibid., p.188.

13. Rutherford, *Riches*, p.94.

14. Rutherford, *World Distress*, p.40.

15. Rutherford, *Riches*, p.188.

16. Rutherford, *Deliverance*, p.222. In *Creation* Rutherford referred to 'pious frauds, called preachers or clergymen'.

17. Pike, op. cit., p.117.

18. Cf. James Black, *New Forms of the Old Faith*, Nelson, London 1948, p.200.

19. Stroup, op. cit., p.63.

FURTHER READING

Bates, E. S., Article on 'Russell, Charles Taze' in *Dictionary of American Biography*, 1931.

Pike, Royston, *Jehovah's Witnesses*, Watts, London, and Philosophical Library, New York 1954.

Rutherford, 'Judge': his chief works are: *Religion, Salvation, Enemies, Riches, Light, Government, Prophecy, Reconciliation, Preservation, Deliverance, The Harp of God* and *Preparation*. His most important pamphlets are perhaps *Theocracy, Armageddon* and *God and the State*.

Stroup, H. H., *The Jehovah's Witnesses*, Columbia University Press, New York 1945.

The Yearbook of the Jehovah's Witnesses, published annually since 1933, gives a useful account of the worldwide activities of the Witnesses.

7 Spiritualism

*Try the spirits whether they be of
God* (I John 4.1)

Spiritualism is belief in the survival of personality beyond death
and that the spirits of the departed actually communicate with the
living. How can the attraction that Spiritualism has for its many
devotees be accounted for? In Britain, as in the United States,
there are Spiritualists who link their beliefs with Christianity and
are known as 'Christian Spiritualists', and others who are agnostic
and refer to themselves solely as 'Spiritualists'. According to the
London *Sunday Times* (24 July 1960) there are about a thousand
Spiritualist centres (perhaps a quarter of them 'Christian') with a
membership of a quarter of a million in Britain. The standard
handbook, the *Yearbook of the American Churches*, lists the
'International General Assembly of Spiritualists' and its address,
but no statistics are now recorded. In the edition of 1964, however,
there were said to be 178,855 Spiritualists in the USA.

Four factors help to account for the attraction of Spiritualism.
The first and the most important is the deep longing for the
bereaved human heart to know whether its beloved dead survive
in another world. It is the men and women who sigh, 'O for the
touch of a vanished hand and the sound of a voice that is still', who
go to spiritualist meetings or seances. It is no cause for wonder that
Spiritualism should flourish in an age which has seen two major
world wars in three decades. One can only have a profound sympathy for those distracted persons who have been twice bereaved
in a lifetime.

The second reason for the success of this movement is that three
figures of national importance in England and one in the United
States were avowed Spiritualists. One was Sir Arthur Conan

Doyle (distinguished novelist and creator of 'Sherlock Holmes', and himself obviously proficient in the analysis of evidence). A second was Sir Oliver Lodge, a most eminent physicist and Vice-Chancellor of Birmingham University, a very open-minded man who endured considerable ridicule for his espousal of Spiritualism. Lord Dowding, formerly of the Royal Air Force in the Second World War, was also a notable enthusiast for Spiritualism. The man who has most recently provided a hearing for Spiritualism in the United States is the famous Episcopal Bishop of California, who believed that a communicator was able to bring him messages from his son who had committed suicide. This has been fully described in the sympathetic work of Hans Holzer, *The Psychic World of Bishop Pike*, 1970. All these men have given Spiritualism the appearance of a trustworthy creed because they subscribed to it. At the same time it should be remembered that Sir Oliver Lodge also condemned some Spiritualistic practice as quackery and superstition.

Success has come to Spiritualism for a third reason, precisely because there is in the public mind a tendency to confuse the non-Christian Spiritualists and the Christian Spiritualists, and therefore to assume that all Spiritualists are Christians who emphasize as their cardinal tenet the Resurrection of Christ, when this is not the case. Such confusion was to be expected when Spiritualist assemblies met in buildings with such names as 'The Church of Christian Fellowship', 'The Temple of the Holy Trinity' or 'The Church of the Spirit'. Despite some similarities in teaching, however, there are radical divergences between even the so-called 'Christian Spiritualists' and historic Christianity.

A fourth reason why Spiritualism is successful is one that appeals particularly to those who are non-Christian Spiritualists. This is the conviction that Spiritualism offers an interpretation of the universe that is optimistic, supposedly based on empirical evidence, and is uncomplicated by theological or ecclesiastical dogmas.

Though this movement has a modern flavour, it has an ancient lineage. In one sense it might be described as a refined form of ancestor worship. It can be traced back to the most primitive form of religion, animism, which attributed souls or spirits to trees, streams and stones. In the dawn of civilization it was customary to explain the eerie and otherwise unaccountable phenomena by recourse to the visitation of the dead. It was fear-engirded, and only a man as desperate as Saul resorted to the witch of Endor to conjure up the dead. The subject was regarded with awesome dread: it was thought to be dangerous and even demonic. In fact, in the Old Testament it was forbidden, and in the New, Simon Magus is one of the most despised figures.

Modern Spiritualism originated in 1847 in Hydeville in the State of New York, with the announcement that strange revelations through mysterious noises and rappings had been made to Margaret and Kate Fox, respectively children of twelve and nine years of age. They claimed that the spirits sent them messages in answer to their questions in a kind of code. Three raps meant an affirmative answer, one rap a negative, and two raps doubtful. The children were pronounced to be mediums, and from a widespread interest in their supposed achievements arose the multiplication of arranged sittings or seances. As a result many mediums took up the occult as a lucrative profession and brought Spiritualism into disrepute. A far more important result, however, was the foundation of the *Society for Psychical Research* in 1882 by an important group of able and sincere scientific investigators. The *Proceedings* of the Society in about sixty volumes constitute the most important record and evaluation of Spiritualist experiences.

I

In justice to Spiritualism it must be acknowledged that its teaching and Christianity have a good deal of common ground. Both agree that man is not merely a complicated body; in fact, both hold that he is a soul in a body. Moreover, both parties to the debate are agreed that individuality survives the disintegration of the body and continues to exercise its faculties. Also, both agree that the Resurrection of Jesus Christ is a reality of the greatest significance.

Furthermore, Spiritualists have insisted that love is the sole and triumphant operative power in the universe, a belief which is closely akin to the claim that God is known as holy love. In addition, there is one article of the Apostles' Creed which both Christians and Spiritualists profess from the heart. It is: 'I believe in the communion of saints.' In the face of contemporary materialism, atheism, agnosticism and nihilism, the importance of these common tenets is considerable and – to this extent at least – Christians can consider Spiritualists as allies.

Some general philosophical parallelism between Spiritualists and Christians can be discerned from the following *Declaration of Principles* issued by the National Spiritualist Association:

1. We believe in Infinite Intelligence.
2. We believe that the phenomena of Nature, both physical and spiritual, are the expression of Infinite Intelligence.
3. We affirm that correct understanding of such expressions and living in accordance therewith constitute true religion.
4. We affirm that the existence and personal identity of the individual continue after the change called death.
5. We affirm that communication with the so-called dead is a fact scientifically proven by the phenomena of Spiritualism.
6. We believe that the highest morality is contained in the Golden Rule...
7. We affirm the moral responsibility of the individual, and that he makes his own happiness or unhappiness as he obeys or disobeys Nature's physical or spiritual laws.
8. We affirm that the doorway to reformation is never closed against any human soul, here or hereafter.[1]

Nonetheless, there are areas of complete divergence between historic and orthodox Christianity which must now be considered.

II

What, then, are these differences and are they important? In general, the differences are both in the manner the information is obtained and in the character and quality of that information itself.

Christianity believes that man is both spiritual and physical. The view is derived by Christians partly from philosophy, but mainly from the life and teaching of Jesus Christ. Christianity's belief in a future life is founded upon God's mighty act in raising Jesus Christ from the tomb and upon Christ's promise, 'If I live, ye shall live also'.

The Spiritualists claim that their information on survival is received from the dead themselves; that is, from controls who are supposed to transmit their messages through a medium in a trance state. This claim cannot by its very nature admit of proof. The dilemma has been admirably stated by Dr Glenn Atkins thus:

> On the one hand, only those beings which are utterly *unknown* to the living anywhere can be finally and conclusively a testimony to communications from the dead. On the other hand, unless the information thus received is *known* to the living, its truth or falsity can never be proved or disproved.[2]

Furthermore, the mediums who claim to be in touch with spirits 'on the other side' are not conspicuously intelligent. Even Sir Oliver Lodge reluctantly describes them as generally 'not particularly able or highly educated folk'. However, not all information comes through mediums; some comes from automatic writing, and that type of information has often seemed the most sober and convincing. Generally, however, it comes by way of a medium. This does cause some bewilderment for the interested Christian. It seems strange that messages should come from such unprepossessing channels of communication. According to our Christian understanding, it looks as if God chooses the finest instruments through which to proclaim his message. The information of Christians is received through faith in a Master of Life, whose words can be challenged, and whose character and teaching force us to admit by their quality that they are a revelation of God's very nature. By contrast, the information of Spiritualists is often, though not always (the notable exception being F. W. H. Myers), received at the hands of a stranger, through the offices of a medium about whom they may know next to nothing.

The second divergence between Spiritualism and Christianity is seen in the nature of that future life which both systems of thought depict. Spiritualists in general claim that the future life is the right and prerogative of man, simply as man. The Christian, however, claims that God alone has immortality and that he confers the privilege of eternal life with him only on those who have tried to do his will. Spiritualists believe in an automatic future life, though there are difference 'planes' in it. Christians believe that eternal life is the gift of God, and that to receive such a gift the individual must fulfil certain moral and spiritual conditions.

Furthermore, as will be seen, the Spiritualist's picture of life after death seems spiritually superficial and even tawdry, compared with the richly meaningful Christian conception of eternity. Christians must repudiate any conception of the after-life which regards it essentially as an automatic rest-cure and not primarily as the blessedness of everlasting fellowship with God and his saints.

III

Furthermore, apart from the general charges just considered, Christianity makes eight specific charges against the beliefs and practices of Spiritualism. Before detailing them, it must again be said that the minority of so-called 'Christian Spiritualists' are less open to these charges to some small degree than the non-Christian Spiritualists who are in the great majority.

The first accusation is that Spiritualism is frequently a selfish philosophy of life. In Bede Frost's pointed epigram, it is often 'a glory for me, not a glory for God religion'. It tries to satisfy the craving for certainty in spiritual matters. It may also appeal to the natural man's desire for a heavenly superannuation on easy terms. It is too comfortable a religion; a Christianity without the Cross. It does not appeal to the heroic motives. For Christ's reminder, 'He that loseth his life for my sake and the gospel's, shall save it', it substitutes as its motto, 'Safety first'.

The balance and realism of the Christian faith is seen in the fact that Christ appeals to both motives. He who said, 'Come unto me all ye that labour and are heavy-laden, and I will give you rest', is also the one who said, 'He that would come after me, let him take up his cross and follow me.' It is true that he promised that his followers should reign with him in everlasting life, but St Paul is true to his Lord in declaring, 'Those who suffer with him shall also reign with him.'

Despite its preferred name of 'Spiritualism', this movement is often a very materialistic religion. This is Christianity's second censure of it. What is so disappointing about Spiritualism is the utterly terrestrial nature of the heaven it offers. Heaven is pictured in purely physical terms in the rhetoric that a Madison Avenue advertising man might use to describe a leisure world for the elderly in Florida; or it is seen as a celestial garden city complete with all modern conveniences. Should the reader think this is a gross exaggeration, let him or her mark the following words which are a record of what the control, Pheneas, is supposed to have told Lady Conan Doyle:

> Your home in the other world is ready for you. There is a round small building in the grounds which is filled with exquisite coloured vibrations into which you go when you want your soul's rejuvenation ... There is an oblong pond round which coloured birds come to drink.

Revelations received by other mediums only confirm the impression that this heaven of the Spiritualists is the projection of tired spirits in search of a spa and a pump-room. The following excerpt, extracted from the handbook to heaven entitled *Spirit Intercourse* is sufficient evidence for the charge:

Summer land is 1,350 miles from the earth; light, 100-110 degrees. Pet animals and birds numerous. Flowers and fruit in rich abundance; habitations of brick and stone interspersed with gardens.

In the same vein the catalogue might be continued to include comfortably furnished apartments, with electricity, hot and cold water, and all the usual conveniences. It might easily be the heavenly Hilton hotel, and one can as easily imagine a sprightly St Peter as receptionist, walking down a central winding staircase in spats, wearing immaculate morning dress, with a carnation in his buttonhole, and a watch-chain on which hangs a bunch of golden keys! This uncelestial cavalcade will not do for Christians.

The third charge against Spiritualism is that its revelation is so untheological – it tells us nothing about God. Communion with God does not seem to be envisaged. Also, the paucity of references to God in the communications of the controls might lead one to believe that God is entirely an afterthought, instead of being the sole conceivable ground and guarantee of the survival beyond death.

A fourth charge against Spiritualism is that it can be a dangerous faith. It is not denied that spirits might have intercourse with human beings. The Bible clearly indicates there are two kinds of spirits – good and evil. Believers are warned: 'Try the spirits, whether they be of God.' And in this connection, Spiritualists themselves admit not only that frauds have taken place in seances, but that evil spirits are occasionally present. The following warning is taken from a book written by a psychic medium, who exercised a spiritualist practice for over twenty years. The book from which it comes is *Voices from the Void* and its author is Mrs Travers Smith (or Hesther Dowden, her maiden name).

If I may venture to advise persons who long to speak once more with persons who have vanished into darkness, I should say it is wise and sane not to make the attempt. The chances against genuine communication are about ten to one: the disappointments and doubts connected with the experiments are great.

This caveat was repeated in a book she published in 1920. There can be little doubt that occult trafficking is dangerous for anxious, excitable or neurotic people, and such investigations should be left in the hands of the accredited societies engaged in psychical experiments. Spiritualism is not only dangerous to sanity, but also a menace to faith. Professor L. W. Grensted offered this wise advice:

> The traffic in signs, the miracle-mongering not for the sake of love but for the sake of the miracle, the quest for manifestations and the rest, can become a most perilous distraction, separating the Spirit alike from God and from the everyday world in which God's work must be done.[3]

At heart Spiritualism is not trust of God; it is born of distrust of him. It is an attempt to substitute experimental certainty for faith. It is an attempt to subject God to the indignity of a test-tube examination. The fifth charge is, then, that Spiritualism is basically scepticism rather than faith.

The sixth count against Spiritualism is that its claims are inconclusive. The most recent careful and objective consideration of the question is Paul Beard's *Survival of Death, For and Against*. The author asserts that 'to obtain evidence concerning survival of death is at once extremely easy and extraordinarily difficult' and that the researcher will find 'that the evidence has in fact produced two quite different answers'. If one takes the answer based on psychical research, then the conclusion is 'that survival is not so far a necessary hypothesis to account for the available evidence'.[4] The second answer is based upon private and personal experiences, which those who had them found quite convincing. While Spiritualism certainly faces us with explaining paranormal phenomena, at least four explanations have been offered to account for phenomena. Some have attributed them to fraud. Others have said they are due to self-deception – the unintended giving away of personal information to the medium or a temporary lapse in concentration or observation on the part of a person attending a seance. Others, again, have attributed the phenomena to a collective unconsciousness into which the medium delves. A most promising explanation connects the phenomena with telepathy – the communication of thoughts from one mind to another without the usual senses. Amid this confusing variety of claims, the only verdict on the claims of the Spiritualists so far must be 'Not proven'.

A seventh charge against Spiritualism is that it contains elements of the suspicious and the ridiculous. G. K. Chesterton has satirized the element of the ridiculous in the sceptical question: 'Do you expect to hear the voice of God calling from a coal-cellar?' (Though the question loses much of its point nowadays when mediums do not work in the dark!) The answer to Chesterton's rhetorical question is that God's voice is heard saying of Jesus, 'This is my beloved Son; hear ye him', and that beloved Son has said, 'In my Father's house are many mansions. I go to prepare a place for you ... If it were not so, 1 would have told you.' Trusting him, the firstborn from the dead, we take his promise on trust. Experiments are unnecessary where faith prevails. For experiences make them unnecessary.

With the poet we may affirm:

> I know not where his islands lift
> Their fronded palms in air;
> I only know I cannot drift
> Beyond his love and care.

That is all we know and possibly all we need to know. A spiritual faith cannot rest upon materialistic proofs. The sole foundation for our belief in eternal life as Christians must be God's promise and 'the exceeding greatness of his power to usward who believe, according to the working of the strength of his might, which he wrought in Christ when he raised him from the dead'.

NOTES

1. Frank S. Mead, *Handbook of Denominations in the United States,* rev. ed., Abingdon Press, New York and Nashville 1956, p.198.
2. Gaius Glenn Atkins, *Modern Religious Cults and Movements,* Allen and Unwin, London, and Fleming Revell, New York 1923, p.313.
3. *Expository Times,* Vol. LIV, p.203.
4. Paul Beard, *Survival of Death,* Hodder and Stoughton, London 1966, pp.3f.

FURTHER READING

The Spiritualist Manual, National Spiritualist Association, Washington, DC.

Beard, Paul, *Survival of Death*, Hodder and Stoughton, London 1966.

Holzer, Hans, *The Psychic World of Bishop Pike*, New York 1970.

Lawton, George S., *The Drama of Life after Death*, Henry Holt, New York 1932.

West, D. J., *Psychical Research Today*, Penguin Books, London 1962.

Thompson, Ernest, *The History of Modern Spiritualism, The Scientific Foundation of Modern Spiritualism*, Manchester 1948.

8 British-Israel

*...the Gentiles are fellow-heirs, and
fellow-members of the body, and fellow-
partakers of the promise in Jesus
Christ through the gospel* (Ephesians 3.6)

I perceive God is no respecter of persons
(Acts 10.34)

*There is neither Jew nor Greek ... Ye
are all one in Christ Jesus. And if ye are
Christ's then ye are Abraham's seed,
heirs according to the promise*
(Galatians 3.28f.)

British-Israel is a theory, rather than a sect or heresy, held by
some two million adherents within the Protestant communions.
British-Israelites hold that the British Commonwealth of nations
and the United States of America are the descendants of the ten
lost tribes of Israel and that they inherit today the political promises made by God to ancient Israel. This theory, like many of
the tenets of the sects, is based upon highly fanciful exegesis of the
Bible.

Protestants have been rightly called 'the people of a book'. This
was expressed most cogently by Chillingworth when he claimed:
'The Bible and the Bible alone is the religion of Protestants.' Today
it would be desirable to amend this definition to indicate that the
Bible was the *basis* of the religion of Protestants. When Martin
Luther dared to criticize the corruptions of the later medieval
church in the West, his only authority was 'The Word of God'.
This alone, he claimed, was an authority higher than the church.
He therefore demanded a 'Reformation according to the Word of
God'. Protestants stand proudly within this great tradition and are
thus obliged to measure all policies by 'the rule of faith' in the
Holy Scriptures. Our faith, our ethics, our liturgy, are inescapably
biblical.

If the Bible is, in fact, the sole doctrinal authority of Protestants,
why are there so many sects amongst Protestants? Here the term
'sects' is to be distinguished from 'denominations', because the

latter accept the scriptures as the supreme rule of faith and life, and differ radically only in their various forms of ecclesiastical government. By the 'sects' is intended the congeries of bodies which have seceded or broken away from the historic Christian churches to establish their own organizations in opposition. Among a vast and variegated array, which includes the Seventh-Day Adventists, Jehovah's Witnesses, Mormons and Russellites, the 'sects' witness to the danger of biblical exegesis uninfluenced by the traditional wisdom and experience of the church of the centuries. When once the Bible was issued to the people, translated into their native tongues, without assistance in its interpretation, they misunderstood parts of it, ignored other sections of it, and often read into it their presuppositions or prejudices. The anthology of the Bible thus compiled by subjectivism was erected into a variety of religious systems for which the authority of the biblical record was claimed.

Such, then, was the peril of private and idiosyncratic interpretation of the scriptures. Equally hazardous was the exclusively literal exegesis of the scriptures. Unfortunately, this danger does not only beset those outside the historic Christian churches; it is often found within them. An instance of ingenious private interpretation, literalist in type, may be given here. Sir James Young Simpson, the distinguished Scottish surgeon, was once thwarted in his attempts to introduce chloroform into gynaecology by a group of 'fundamentalist' ministers of religion, who urged the authority of the creation text, 'In sorrow and labour shalt thou bring forth thy children.' His retort out-literalized the literalists, by claiming that he had divine authority in the same narrative for the use of anaesthetics, for God had put Adam 'into a deep sleep' before removing his rib. This apparent digression is relevant to the study of British-Israel, for this is a theory based upon private and often crassly literalist misinterpretations of the Bible.

I

The claims of British Israelitism must now be considered. The necessary information on the principles of the British-Israel World Federation may be found in two of their authoritative compilations. One is a pamphlet by Commander Studd, entitled *Britain's Place in Prophecy*, and the other, *The Heritage of the Anglo-Saxon Race*, by M. H. Gayer, OBE.

From a perusal of these expositions, it appears that British-

Israelites hold three basic beliefs. First, they maintain that the Old Testament prophecies made by God to Abraham and confirmed to his descendants must be literally and materially fulfilled. In the second place, they hold that these promises and subsequent prophecies require for their fulfilment a belief that the ten tribes of the northern kingdom of Israel must have persisted as a nation, ruled by a king of the Davidic dynasty. Thirdly, they claim that Britain, the British Empire and the United States of America are the inheritors of the promises of God because they are the descendants of the ten lost tribes of Israel, and because Britain is ruled by a monarch of the Davidic line.

The last hypothesis they attempt to establish in an ingenious, if unconvincing, manner. The ten tribes, they maintain, were taken captive by the Assyrians in the eighth century BC. From captivity they wandered over Europe as the Scythians, Cimmerians and Goths. From Europe they invaded England as the Angles, Saxons, Jutes and Normans, commingling their blood with that of the Ancient Britons. Therefore, they insist, the citizens of Britain, the British Commonwealth and the Americans are the inheritors of the divine promises to Abraham and constitute the New Israel, the master-nation. A summary of this fanciful reconstruction of ethnology is provided by one of their own writers:

> Getae, Massagetae, Sacae, Scythians, Goths, Ostro-Goths, Dacians, Khumri, Milesians, Danes, Jutes, Angles, Saxons, Normans – with many another name that could be added – all at last, either by trade or simple migration, but mostly by fierce fighting and conquest the one or the other found their way into these 'Isles of the West'. They were 'sifted among the nations', as God said they would be, but not a 'grain' has been lost, and out of them all have truly evolved the English, Scotch, Irish, Welsh of the British Empire, and the American of the United States.[1]

If their ethnology is fanciful, their philology is fantastic! 'Saxon' is interpreted as 'Saac's sons' and therefore means Isaac's sons, thus fulfilling God's promise of Genesis 21.12: 'In Isaac shall thy seed be called.' No less far-fetched is the derivation of 'British' from *berithish*, *berith* being the Hebrew for 'covenant' and *ish* the Hebrew for 'man', i.e. men of the covenant. Fantasy goes even further in claiming that 'John Bull' was so named because Isaac's British sons sacrificed the bullock, which in Hebrew is spelled *engle*, hence 'England'.[2]

The foundation-stone of the entire edifice of British-Israel is the belief that the promises and prophecies of the Old Testament must be fulfilled literally. Otherwise, it is suggested, God is made to appear a liar and a breaker of his word. One important point, however, seems to be ignored. That is, that nowhere in his word does God declare that his promises are to be fulfilled to the letter. It is, in fact, quite impossible to discover a literal meaning in much of the scriptures. Why, therefore, should the promises be interpreted literally and not metaphorically? Scripture has not always a simple, straightforward meaning, any more than everyday speech has.

One instance of the folly of interpreting common parlance literally may be given, for in this respect God's parlance (the Word of God) is analogous. Let us suppose that a young man has recently become engaged, and that his ecstasy finds expression in a love-letter by a quotation from a lyric. He writes to his fiancée that 'My love is like a red, red rose'. He does not imply by this description that she is a ruddy-cheeked country lass with a florid complexion. Nor is this a subtle way of declaring that she is lovely, but her loveliness will fade and wither with the years. Least of all does he mean that her apparently sweet disposition has unsuspected cruelty lurking beneath it, as thorns below the rose. His meaning (or rather *one* of the layers of meaning) is that as the rose is lovely, so is she. The meaning is metaphorical, not literal.

The Bible frequently uses this metaphorical, short-hand type of speech – these implicit similes. For instance, Jesus says, 'I am the light of the world.' This cannot mean that he is the sun, but that his person and message bring illumination to the souls of men darkened by sin. When he says, 'I am the door', it cannot be interpreted as meaning that the composition of his body is wood. His meaning is that, as a door gives entry to a house, so does he open the kingdom of heaven to all believers.

The same test should be applied to the promises of God to Abraham and his seed. One example of over-facile British-Israelite exegesis may be considered. God made the following promise to Jacob. 'I will multiply thy seed as the sand which is upon the sea-shore.' The following is Commander Studd's interpretation of this passage:

They were to be numerous as the sand of the sea, suggesting at least a great sea-faring nation.[3]

Does the text suggest that Israel shall be a sea-faring nation?

There is not a hint of it. In addition, it seems that Israel had no trace of sea-fever in its history, for when Solomon built a port to the north of the Gulf of Akaba for his joint mercantile enterprises with Hiram, the Phoenician ruler, his fleet had to be manned with Tyrian sailors. The text simply asserts that Jacob's descendants shall be as numerous as the grains of sand upon the sea-shore. The prophetic 'hint' of a sea-faring nation originates in the noble Commander's fertile brain, not in the Bible. We might suggest that the Commander is viewing the scriptures through the telescope of the Royal Navy; it is even possible that, like Nelson, he puts a blind eye to the telescope! This is but one apposite example of exegesis that fails by literalizing a metaphor.

Two other texts which are used for the 'sanctified imperialism' of the British variety are Jer. 25.22, 'the isle beyond the sea', which is interpreted as meaning Britain; and it is said that the promise made to Abraham in Gen. 22.17, 'Thy seed shall possess the gate of his enemies', refers particularly to the British possessions of Gibraltar, Malta, Cyprus and Suez! In fact the literal meaning of the word translated as 'isle' in the former citation is, as the marginal reading in the Revised Version indicates, 'coastland', and the word translated as 'gates' in the latter citation is simply 'cities'. Clearly, this is exegetical ignorance masquerading as originality.

Such fanciful exegesis must be censured, but it does not dispose of the larger questions: How were the promises to Abraham and his seed fulfilled? The New Testament, nevertheless, does dispose of this question in several places. It claims that the promises and prophecies made by God to the chosen people are fulfilled in Jesus Christ and his community, the New Israel. St Paul, for example, declares: 'The Gentiles are fellow-heirs and fellow-members of the body, and fellow-partakers of the promise in Christ Jesus through the gospel.' Elsewhere, referring to Christ, St Paul writes, 'In him are all the promises of God.' In yet another place he states categorically, 'And if ye are Christ's, then are ye Abraham's seed, heirs according to the promise.'

St Peter may also be summoned as a witness to the truth that the promises of God to Abraham are fulfilled in the Christian church. He says, in a sermon preached to the Jews but with an eye on the Gentiles, 'Ye are the children of the prophets, and of the covenant which God made with our fathers, saying unto Abraham, And in thy seed shall all the families of the earth be blessed. Unto you *first* God, having raised up his Son Jesus, sent him to bless you, in turning every one of you from his iniquities' (Acts 3.25-6). Clearly it is the church which inherited the fulfilment of the promises in Christ. The church had comparatively few converts from Judaism, but many Gentiles within its fold. The fulfilment of the promises was not biologically conceived, as the British-Israelites claim it ought to have been. It was a spiritual fulfilment. Since the majority of the chosen people rejected Jesus the Messiah, they had forfeited the promises.

Because these promises were spiritually fulfilled in Christ and conveyed to his faithful followers, regardless of nationality or race, it is unnecessary to look for any biological fulfilment. This being the case, the second and third principles of British-Israel are ruled out of court. Since the promises were spiritually fulfilled and are available for all Christians, it is superfluous to search for evidence of the history of the lost ten tribes of Israel. Because the fulfilment of Abraham's promises has taken place in the kingdom of God over which Christ rules as King of kings and Lord of lords, we need not look to the future for the realization of the divine promises to Abraham.

II

If the biblical interpretation of the British-Israelites is eccentric and their re-writing of history chimerical, how can their appeal be accounted for? Several factors play an important part in the attraction of British-Israel. First, it appeals to patriotic people, who find a biblical warrant for the importance of their nation in the affairs of the world. One might go further and say that it is peculiarly attractive to those who believe themselves to be the *Herrenvolk*.

Secondly, it appeals to persons perplexed by the maze of history, who are searching for a philosophy of history which will counteract the apparent insignificance of individuals on the modern scene. To such the Bible offers a key to world-history.

In the third place, they are unconsciously seeking for an adequate doctrine of the church as the new Israel of God, believing that God calls peoples, not merely individual units, into his service.

This threefold appeal is a solemn warning for the churches. They must be more careful to instruct their charges that the international and interracial church of Christ has claims that override even patriotism. The churches must learn from the idiosyncratic exegesis of the British-Israelites the need for sounder biblical instruction. It seems, in Professor J. R. Coates's phrase, that many within the churches look upon the Word of God 'as a sort of time-table in cypher'.[4] Christians are particularly ignorant of the philosophy of the apocalyptic books of the Bible, which are such a happy hunting-ground for sectarians and schismatics.

III

A detailed critique of British-Israel must now be offered. Our first criticism is that, since New Testament days, the need for an elect nation has disappeared, for it has been met by the inter-national church of Christ. The final Word of God in the New Testament is that racial distinctions are irrelevant in the matter of salvation. There is no suggestion in it that there can be a master-race. Christ's great mission to the world will be fulfilled by individuals nurtured in community, who will gather up other individuals to whom they have proclaimed the gospel into com-munities. Such individuals and communities created and confirmed by the gospel, whatever the race or races included in their member-ship, are Christ's chosen people, the church.

Christ is Messiah of all nations alike, and as all nations may be chosen, there is no need for a particular chosen nation. In the re-deemed community or race all distinction of nationality, class, race, sex and culture are transcended, for 'there is neither Jew nor Greek, circumcision nor uncircumcision, barbarian, Scythian, bond nor free: but Christ is all in all'. The renascence of doctrines of a privileged race have proved in recent times dangerous to the peace of the nations, and a poison in the veins of the body of Christ, the church. Such teaching, it cannot be too often insisted upon, is a flat denial of the gospel doctrine. It disregards the words of John the Baptist, 'begin not to say within yourselves, We have Abraham to our father'. It refuses to consider seriously St Paul's saying, 'he is not a Jew which is one outwardly'. It contradicts outright the solemn declaration of Jesus himself, 'the flesh profiteth nothing'.

It could also be pointed out that the British-Israelites entirely misunderstand the nature of 'election' even in the old covenant, for God chose the Israelites for service, not for privilege. This was the bitter reminder of the prophecy of Amos, 'You only have I known of all the families of the earth: therefore I will visit upon you all your iniquities.' In the deepest thought of the Old Testament the doctrine of election was expanded in its charity to include uni-versalism: 'Are ye not as the children of the Ethiopians unto me, O children of Israel? saith the Lord. Have not I brought up Israel out of the land of Egypt, and the philistines from Caphtor, and the Syrians from Kir?' (Amos 9.7). The British-Israelites are anachronisms.

In the second place, they must be accused of imperfectly understanding the nature and authority of the Bible, as their faulty exegesis proves. Whether they deal with the law, the prophets, the writings, the gospels or the epistles, they place them on the same level as instructors in Christian doctrine. The Old Testament is more important to them than the New, with the exception of the Book of Revelation. The inspiration of the Bible is not all on the same level: the Bible itself is, in Luther's phrase, the 'cradle of Christ' and the Old Testament must be judged by the revelation of the word of God Incarnate, the mind of Christ.

They must be censured for regarding the prophets as prediction-experts. The prophets did not come among the people to foretell distant events; they were there to foretell God's will for their own generation. This distinction is admirably made by Professor J. E. McFadyen in *The Bible and Modern Thought*:

> No one who reads such a book as Amos could carry away the impression that its importance lay in prediction. Running through it, doubtless, is the broad announcement that national sin will issue in national ruin, but the value of this lies in its moral interpretation of history, not in its miraculously predictive quality.

Furthermore, British-Israelite exegesis unwarrantably distinguishes between the fulfilment of passages referring to Israel and those referring to Judah. We may well ask: why should the divine promises made to the whole people apply only to the relatively small segment of the nation which was carried into captivity?

In the third place, the whole import and emphasis of British-Israel leads to a false sense of racial security, to a dangerous racial pride and an unworthy conception of God. Of this implication of their teaching Dr James Black has said:

> British-Israel theory ... is dangerously like some modern theories of race superiority which have only brought sorrow, shame and insolence into men's hearts. Quite seriously, I regard this type of idea as one of the dangers to human peace and sanity.[5]

Fourthly and finally, it must be stated that the subsidiary historical, ethnological and philological arguments used by the champions of British-Israel are contrary to the ascertained facts and are often fantastically improbable. No reputable archaeologist would be found to agree that the Scythians were of Semitic origin, as there are no traces of Semitic influence on either their language or their customs. The ethnological link in the British-Israelite historical chain is so weak that Israel's most distinctive customs – circumcision, seventh-day observance, ritual cleanness – have not survived amongst the Scythians, Cimmerians, Angles, Saxons or Celts. We are informed that the languages of the United Kingdom contain many words akin to Hebrew, but a glance at the *Concise Oxford Dictionary* would explode the delightful philological balloons. Expert philologists assure us that there are no possible links in vocabulary, grammar or syntax between the Semitic language of the ten tribes and the Low or High German of the Teutons.

The crux of the whole theory is historical. But many other claims for the lost ten tribes have been made. The Mormons urge that the Indians of North America are they, while other peoples that have been suggested for the same role are the Laplanders and the Mexicans. The joint editor of Valentine's *Jewish Encyclopedia* maintains that there are only two claims for descent from the lost tribes which have any serious basis, namely those of the Afghans and the Nestorians.

IV

It would be unsatisfactory to let the matter end there. With the British-Israelites we must also recognize that God fulfils his purpose through nations as well as through individuals, though it is the individuals which determine the character of a nation. Nations, as well as individuals, may be the instruments of the divine justice punishing aggressors. The Old Testament indicates that God may anoint nations other than his chosen people Israel, to be the instruments of judgment on his chosen but impenitent people. For this reason Elijah could speak of Hazael, whom he anointed as king of Syria, as God's agent; similarly, but in more direct fashion, a later prophet could speak of the king of Persia, as seen by God, in the following words: 'Thus saith the Lord to his anointed, to Cyrus ... I will gird thee though thou hast not known me' (Isa. 45.1). Isaiah (10.5) says, 'O Assyrian, the rod of my anger ...' implying that God's will is made effectual through other nations of the world. Similarly, the dark signature of divine displeasure was written over the ruined cities of Europe. But the nations whom

God selects to fulfil his purposes are never master-races; they are servant-races – they exist in order to obey the behests of the Almighty. It is an election to responsibility and even to suffering, as Israel knew of old. No nation is elected by God to lord it over other peoples, as a *Herrenvolk* or imperial régime.

In this strictly limited sense, when to suffer oppression would be worse than to draw the bloody sword of justice, nations may be the agents of divine justice, though never as self-appointed agents. Nations as well as individuals can fall a prey to hypocrisy and Pharisaism. In this sense also, nations that inherit the traditions of a Christian civilization – the so-called 'Christian countries' – are under obligation to protect and perpetuate the Christian faith, and are thus elected.

But the Bible speaks of another sword, more effectual than the sword of justice; it is the sword of the Spirit, the word of God. This alone will provide the basis for communal and international integration. Justice is founded upon the threat of coercion, but the sword of the Spirit is love. Men can be cowed into terror by the sword of justice or war, and when men and nations neglect or spurn the rights of individuals and of other nations, the last recourse of the defenders of divine justice may be this ugly weapon of fear. But lasting unity among the nations becomes possible only when men see the love of God in the Cross of Christ stooping to conquer, embracing man in his loathsomeness and setting him on his feet again. Such divine reconciliation is the only enduring basis of international comity.

The Christian's task is therefore to vanquish the rebellious hearts of men by the weakest thing in the world – the wounds of a crucified King. But the weakness of God is stronger than the power of men, as his folly is wiser than the sagacity of men.

NOTES

1. L. Sapsworth, *The Bible Arch of British-Israel Truth,* R. Banks & Son, London 1910, p.94.

2. Ralph Lord Roy, *Apostles of Discord,* Beacon Press, Boston, 1953, p.96.

3. *Britain's Place in Prophecy,* p.6.

4. *Expository Times,* Vol. LIV, p.315.

5. James Black, *New Forms of the Old Faith,* Nelson, London 1948, p.282.

FURTHER READING

Allen, J. H., *Judah's Sceptre and Joseph's Birthright*, Destiny Publishers, 13th ed., Haverhill, Mass. 1941.

Gayer, M. H., *The Heritage of the Anglo-Saxon Race*, Destiny Publishers, Haverhill, Mass. 1941.

felders, a pietistical group with a strong belief in the direct illumination by God of the human soul. This, so Driberg asserts with considerable probability, may be the origin of Buchman's conviction of the reality of divine guidance.[3] He received the usual training for the Lutheran ministry. It was begun at Muhlenberg College in Allentown and completed at Mount Airy Theological Seminary on the outskirts of Philadelphia. His first charge was the impoverished Lutheran congregation in Overbrook in his native state, whither he had deliberately gone because a college friend had accused him of overweening personal ambition. Here he founded a boys' settlement and later resigned his charge after a disagreement with the trustees. He then became a dynamic YMCA secretary at Pennsylvania State University.

A distinguished Lutheran church historian, Dr Theodore Tappert, believes that the formative influences on Dr Buchman and, therefore, on the future Oxford Group, are 'a combination of pietism and the YMCA movement', and that 'the emphasis on a sharp conversion experience' was typical of the Lutheran pietism of the eighteenth century which he inherited. If to this we add the Schwenkfeldian emphasis on divine and direct guidance, and American advertising technique, as well as the evangelical reinforcement which Buchman received while at a Keswick convention in England, these would seem to be the essential components of the earlier phase of the Oxford Group Movement. It would not, perhaps, be unfair to describe Dr Buchman as a vigorous exponent of dynamic moralistic pietism. Such a phrase is not intended in any pejorative sense, but as a term which defines the intense personal devotion to Christ, the insistence upon rigorous moral standards, and the conviction that the real church consists of warmed hearts committed to witness – the *ecclesiola* or 'little church' within the church.

Because he had found peace of mind by submitting his own will to the will of God, he was convinced that religion was not essentially a matter of the intellect, nor even of the heart, but of the will. His life's work would be dedicated to persuading others to live by the will of God, through sharing his own experience. The element of the confession of sins and victory over them became paramount in his thinking at this time. With his characteristic gift for terse and telegrammatic utterance, he summed it up as follows: 'The degree of our freedom from sin is the degree of our desire to be free.' The pietism was expressed in two age-old but newly rediscovered techniques: 'sharing' and 'guidance' with the purpose of 'life-changing'. 'Sharing' was, in fact, the confession of sins, either privately or before a small group, which marked the reality of repentance and the new beginning of the Christian life. It also took the positive form of mutual encouragement in the victory over past failures. The moralism was mixed with the pietism in the technique of 'guidance'. It was believed that the new life in Christ must be marked by the 'four absolutes': absolute honesty, absolute purity, absolute unselfishness and absolute love, and that for those gathered for their 'quiet time' God would provide detailed directions for the duties of each day. The religious discipline for attaining these rigoristic four absolutes was described as follows:

1. The Sharing of our sins and temptations with another Christian life given to God, and to use Sharing as witness to help others, still unchanged, to recognize and acknowledge their sins.
2. Surrender of our life, past, present, and future, into God's keeping and direction.
3. Restitution to all whom we have wronged directly or indirectly.
4. Listening to, accepting, relying on God's Guidance and carrying it out in everything we do or say, great or small.[4]

In the disenchantment of the post-war years in England, as in the ironically-named 'gilded age' of the United States, there was a vacuum of the soul which Buchman proceeded to fill with Christian convictions and moral standards. His meetings were characterized by the brilliant informality of 'house-parties', so that the movement became what has been called 'the Salvation Army of the middle classes'.

The first house-party was held in Kuling in China, in 1918, at the home of a prominent lawyer, and was attended by over a hundred guests.

In 1921 there was organized 'A First Century Christian Fellowship', under which name the movement was first known. The name 'Oxford Group' was first used in South Africa by newspapermen in 1929 and from 1934 onwards it was regularly employed. The change to 'Moral Re-Armament' which may have been presaged in a speech of Buchman's at East Ham Town Hall on 29 May 1938, came to the forefront in the Second World War and after. This represented at least a partial change of outlook and activity. While 'God-control' and 'life-changing' were still stressed, the main thrust of the propaganda of the movement was now on providing

an ideology to equip democracy for its struggle against materialism in general, and dialectical materialism (Communism) in particular. Although this diminution of emphasis on the specifically
Christian and evangelical character of the earlier movement is
officially denied, yet it is difficult to see how an ideology for democracy which is commended to Shintoists and Buddhists in Japan,
and to Hindus and Buddhists in India and Ceylon, can be anything
but vaguely theistic, far less Christocentric. It is precisely this later
preference for an ideology for democracy, in lieu of the older and
simpler Christian revivalism with some social sophistication, which
raises the greatest question as to the Christian nature of Moral Re-
Armament today.

The chief centres of Moral Re-Armament are to be found in a
complex of hotels in Caux, Switzerland, in the impressive Mack-
inac Island off the shores of Lake Michigan in the USA, and in
Odowara, in central Japan. One of the most interesting developments is the use of the Westminster Theatre in London for the
putting-on of MRA plays which have often gone on tour in various
parts of the world. Amongst the most widely seen of such propaganda plays are *The Forgotten Factor, The Good Road*, and *Give
a Dog a Bone*, chiefly the work of an imaginative journalist, Peter
Howard. Here again there is an ingenious revival of an old Christian technique, developed in the medieval morality and miracle
plays and resuscitated in the distinguished Canterbury plays written for and promoted by the Church of England, of which four
eminent examples were T. S. Eliot's *Murder in the Cathedral*,
Dorothy L. Sayers' *The Zeal of Thy House* and Christopher Fry's
The Lady's Not for Burning and *The Sleep of Prisoners*.

Of the ingenuity of the MRA there is no question, nor of its
capacity to attract many lapsed or nominal Christians as well as
non-Christians. The real question is whether its present core of
Christian leaders are committed to the historic and incarnation-
centred faith (or some increasingly diluted and moralistic version
of it) and whether they are commando forces of the church or
diversionary ideological deviationists.[5]

II

Moral Re-Armament has undoubtedly many advantages that commend it to the modern world, and it has developed or revived tech-

niques for commending its views, some of which might well be imitated by the historic churches today.

There must be appreciation, deep appreciation, for any movement which in the present era of ethical relativity makes a valiant stand for the moral values of our Judaeo-Christian civilization in the West and for spiritual brotherhood in the East. If MRA were still more obviously tied to its pietistical Christian origins than appears to be the case in its recent ideological phase, much more could be said on its behalf. For example, its stress on the conversion of the individual as proven in the 'changed' life with its concomitant demand for restitution to those wronged, for the witness of 'sharing', and for the devotion of time and money in the cause, were all admirable.

It has (or had) a gift for terse and relevant 'translation' of the terms of the Christian faith and life into modern speech. The attempt to do this has been wholly admirable, even though the achievement has, as is natural, often suffered from slickness or a spurious simplicity. One is not entirely convinced with the assurance that this was 'milk for babes', because there is little evidence that the babes are encouraged to grow up to appreciate the 'strong meat of the gospel'. But this is surely better than to rely on outworn phrases and clichés, as Christian orthodoxy has so often done.

Moral Re-Armament has discovered or rediscovered useful new techniques for commending its convictions. The strategy of house-parties, of public meetings for testimony, and the use of religious drama are three very potent examples of ingenious initiative.

In recent years MRA has paid great attention to the attempt (without radical socio-economic reorganization) to solve industrial and political conflicts across class and racial barriers, with some degree of success. Many well-known labour leaders and parliamentarians, as well as statesmen, have either associated themselves with the movement or spoken on its platforms. Undoubtedly, one of the greatest reasons for the interest in the MRA has been its public posture as the defender of a moral ideology as an alternative to Communism in the West.

Finally, the newcomer (unless he is an impenitent introvert) is bound to be impressed by the *camaraderie* of the MRA, its sense of commitment to the cause, and the disciplined and dedicated lives of its supporters. Cumulative, these characteristics of the movement are, at least in part, sufficient to account for its success. They also help to explain the ambiguity of its status by which it is both lauded and criticized by different leaders and members of many branches of the Christian church.

III

All human movements, however august their claims to Divine origination, inspiration and support, are *mixed* communities. It has hitherto counted severely against the Oxford Group and MRA that however much this has been admitted privately, the public posture was that of an infallible perfectionist organization, inordinately sensitive to criticism. It was, therefore, all the more welcome that the Rev. J. P. Thornton-Duesbery in *The Open Secret of M.R.A.* openly admitted the fallibility of the movement. 'There are,' he wrote, 'imperfections in MRA. There were in Buchman, as he was himself the first to admit. MRA is no panacea for every human ill, although there *is* a panacea as we shall presently see.' He continued this open-minded admission, with what the present writer can only concede is a sincere but exaggerated claim, that 'my years of observation have steadily strengthened my conviction that, whatever its shortcomings, the Hand of God is upon it and in it, and that to miss the sight of this is to miss perhaps the most significant and hopeful feature of this critical time'.[6] The admission of fallibility makes possible the opening of a genuine dialogue between MRA and the historic Christian churches. With this may be coupled the concluding sentence of Driberg's book: 'If, then, we can learn from them, perhaps it is not too arrogant to wish that they in turn might, now and then, feel disposed to learn something from us.'

It is, then, in preparation for such a dialogue that it is appropriate for members of the historic Christian churches to put some questions to MRA. This will be attempted in the present chapter in briefest and most direct way in the form of a series of questions asking for further illumination from MRA.

1. While acknowledging that truth, honesty, unselfishness and love are the fruits (though not the only fruits) of the Holy Spirit, do you sufficiently allow for the primacy of the Christian virtue of humility?

2. While rightly acknowledging that the Christian faith and way of life is to be a present possession, do you also stress that there is a Christian hope of everlasting life?

3. While properly confessing that Christianity is the acknowledgment of God's rule and reign in personal life, do you also

emphasize that this will also require profound changes in the political, social, and economic structures of society, so that individual patronage shall give way to social justice?

4. While rightly insisting that 'good news' must be proclaimed by word and by transformed life, do you sufficiently distinguish between the commendation of the gospel because it is true, and the commendation of the gospel because of its by-products, such as interior security or morale-building?

5. While rightly perceiving that rationality may be the means of denying or postponing the claim of God on human life, do you also fully allow for the place of honest doubt and for the unhampered discussion of theological and sociological perspectives differing from your own official MRA viewpoint?

6. While rightly recognizing the power for good which 'key' people may exercise when 'changed', do you consider that the advertisement of 'success stories' in your official propaganda may not be in accordance with the gospel precept to avoid ostentation, so that your left hand may not know what your right hand is doing?

7. In rightly recognizing the importance of the 'little church' within the larger church, have you not underestimated the significance of the theological, liturgical, and ethical traditions of the world-spanning and centuries-transcending body of Christ of which all present communions are branches?

8. Can you consistently commend a once Christocentric faith to the West with a merely moral ideology to the East and claim to be Christian in any commonly accepted theological (as contrasted with an ethical) sense? Is is a *theology* or an *ideology* that you ultimately stand for?

It should also be made clear that MRA will have its own questions to ask about the timid, lethargic, custom-bound, and chill levels of Christian obedience in many communions. These, too. should be welcomed in any genuine attempt at dialogue as the honest prelude to a possible reconciliation.

NOTES

1. Tom Driberg, *The Mystery of Moral Re-Armament,* Secker and Warburg, London 1964, p.305.
2. J. P. Thornton-Duesbery, *The Open Secret of M.R.A.,* Blandford Press, London 1964, p.7. Note the transition from a military to a 'big-game hunting' metaphor!
3. Driberg, op. cit., pp.21f.
4. The Layman with a Notebook, *What is the Oxford Group?,* Oxford University Press 1933, p.7.

5. While one may accept the claim of the Rev. J. P. Thornton-Duesbery that the veterans of the MRA from Oxford Group days are a Christian core leadership, there is great point in Driberg's question: 'Whether it can still be classified as a Christian movement or sect, it is clear that MRA has become primarily a morale-building and propagandist instrument in the Cold War' (op. cit., p.150).

6. Thornton-Duesbery, op. cit., p.21. I should have thought the liturgical movement, the development of Christian social thinking and action, and the achievements of the ecumenical movement (Roman Catholic, Orthodox, Anglican and Protestant) were far more significant as hopeful signs than seeing 'the Hand of God' in MRA.

FURTHER READING

Buchman, Frank N. D., *Remaking the World* (speeches), Blandford Press, rev. ed., London 1961; *Frank Buchman: Eighty,* Blandford Press, London 1959.

Driberg, Tom, *The Mystery of Moral Re-Armament,* Secker and Warburg, London 1964.

Howard, Peter, *Ideas Have Legs,* Frederick Muller, London 1945; *Frank Buchman's Secret,* Heinemann, London 1961.

Marcel, Gabriel (ed.), *Fresh Hope for the World,* Longmans, London 1960.

Thornton-Duesbery, J. P., *The Oxford Group: A Brief Account of its Principles and Growth,* Moral Re-Armament, London 1947; *The Open Secret of M.R.A.,* Blandford Press, London 1964.

Williamson, Geoffrey. *Inside Buchmanism,* Watts, London 1954.

10 Theosophy

*Beware of anyone getting hold of you
by means of a theosophy which is
specious make-believe, on the lines of
human tradition, corresponding to
the elemental spirits of the world and
not to Christ* (Colossians 2.8)

Part of the attraction of Theosophy is to be found in its impressive
title. Originally the name meant no more than 'a knowledge of
things divine', a designation which each other religion might claim
for its own. In time, however, it came to carry overtones of meaning, implying that this was a superior and unusually intimate
knowledge of God, reserved only for the intellectually and spiritually advanced. It further suggested that this esoteric system of
doctrines and rites was occult and reserved only for the initiated.
Its first appeal, therefore, is clearly to the pride of the select
intellect.

The other attractions of Theosophy are, it seems, to defend the
justice of the moral order, to offer a prospect of spiritual progress
here and hereafter, and its profession to deliver its devotees from
all constricting theological or ecclesiastical loyalties.

The renewal of interest in Theosophy is also related to the contemporary interest in Buddhism among intellectuals and 'beatniks'.
Its gentle scepticism and deep compassion for all creatures, as well
as its inspiration of some *outré* forms of art, all contribute to make
it attractive to those who seek the unusual and the esoteric.

Although it originates from the time of the mystery religions and
the Gnostics, its contemporary form has a modern derivation. It
commenced when the Theosophical Society was founded by
Madame Blavatsky and Colonel Olcott in New York in 1875. The
Society was intended to compare the methods of Spiritualism with
those of the old Jewish and Egyptian Cabbalas. America proving
too pragmatic and deficient in the appreciation of mysticism,
Madame Blavatsky went to India in 1878 where she gained an

immediate and widespread success. She gathered a group of enthusiastic Indian and European disciples around her and together they studied the speculations of the Eastern mystics. She claimed to be in touch with the Great White Brotherhood of Tibet who were, in her own words, a 'Lodge of Masters or Adepts' in the spiritual life. The Society for Psychical Research investigated this claim but pronounced it fraudulent. After this exposure in 1885, she left Madras. In the ensuing six years of her life, she produced her book, *Secret Doctrine*, which is the catechism of modern Theosophy. This body of teaching was later systematized and developed by Mrs Annie Besant, who gained a respectful hearing for Theosophy among intelligent and cultured people. G. K. Chesterton's recipe for Theosophy aptly summarizes its origin: 'Asia and Evolution and the English lady; and I think they would be better apart.'

It is important to notice that the cult originated in India. The Easterner and the Westerner look through the world with different eyes. The man of the East is naturally a mystic: he is more interested in the inner world of meditation than in the outward world of phenomena and investigation. His religion is apt to be an escape from the world to God. Indeed, he claims to find God by premature retirement from the world.

By contrast, the religion of the man of the West is more a desire to remould the world according to the divine plan. Edward Vernon declares that the symbol of the East is the temple, while the symbol of the West is the scientific laboratory. The East looks inward, the West outward. Or, in psychological terms, the man of the East is an introvert, while the man of the West is an extrovert. Perhaps, however, the best distinction drawn between East and West in religion is Chesterton's. 'The Buddhist saint,' he said, 'has his eyes shut, whilst the Christian saint has his eyes open.' Theosophy, although it claims to be the universal religion, is very much the product of the East, living in the atmosphere of introspection, asceticism and withdrawal from the world which characterizes the religions of the East.

The Theosophical Society today considers itself 'an absolutely unsectarian body of seekers after Truth, striving to serve humanity and revive the religious spirit.' It has three decided aims: (1) To form a nucleus of the Universal Brotherhood of Humanity, without distinction of race, creed, sex, caste or colour. (2) To encourage the study of Comparative Religion, Philosophy and Science. (3) To investigate unexplained laws of Nature and the powers latent in man.

I

The claims of Theosophy must now be considered, especially its implicit belief in karma and reincarnation. As previously indicated, its chief claim is to be the universal religion. Had it not borrowed its doctrines almost exclusively from the East, the claim might have some truth in it. In fact, however, the idea of the unknowability of God derives from the Hindu *Upanishads*, the ideal of detachment from an illusory world is borrowed from Buddhism, as also the doctrine of successive human reincarnations. Furthermore, its methods of attaining to religious peace are all of Eastern origin.

Its claim to be the universal religion cannot be accepted for two other reasons. One is that a religion for spiritual experts only is bound to appeal to a minority, never to the majority, as a universal religion must do. But the most compelling reason against the belief that it is the universal religion is that syncretism takes place only at the cost of destroying all that is distinctive in differing religions. Christianity and Buddhism, for example, will not mix. The Christian ideal of the future life is the perfection of the self, the Buddhist the annihilation of all selfhood.

The second major claim of Theosophy is to be a compound of modern science and ancient philosophy. This is rapidly disposed of by Dr James Black, as he argues that:

> The Eastern speculation of reincarnation, i.e. souls after death being reborn into another human life, is totally against the proved findings of the science of heredity, where offsprings are known to inherit not only their physical life, but also their powers and capabilities from their parents and ancestry.[1]

II

The doctrines of Theosophy can be viewed from three vantage-points.

The teaching about God. Theosophists are pantheists. In their own words: 'All that is is God, and God is all that is.' This insistence upon the unity of God seems to be admirable, until it is examined. When pushed to its logical conclusion, however, its absurdity is patent. If God is everything and everything is God, then God is as much in an archangel as in an atom-bomb, as much in the sunset as in the seaweed, as much in a cherub as in a crocodile, as much in ameliorative medicine as in a microbe, and as much in a martyr as in a mosquito.

But, the Theosophist hastens to explain, all these things were created by God and God wills them to exist. It is true that they are the materials for our human struggle, the fulcrum for our spiritual leverage; but it is idle to pretend that God is indifferent as to whether the microbe slays the man, or the man slays the microbe. Then the Theosophist replies scathingly, 'But you are mistaken. It is foolish to describe God as personal. Would you endow God with the limitations of a finite human personality? He is neither interested nor disinterested, because God is not a he at all. He is suprapersonal.'

It is here that the argument breaks off, because the term 'God' is interpreted differently by the Christian and the Theosophist. What the Christian regards as the noblest way of defining God, the Theosophist takes as an insult to his Deity. If both Christian and Theosophist regard the world as a prison-house, there the agreement ends. The Theosophist is eagerly searching for a key with which to escape. The Christian, on the other hand, is thinking of the other poor spirits confined in the same prison. He is eager to transform convicts into reformed characters. The Christian's greatest stimulus to reformation is the belief that Christ demands that he love his neighbour as himself. He is the brother for whom Christ died. For the Christian, therefore, the world is neither good nor bad; it is neutral. It is the school of character, 'the vale of soul-making', the edge which sharpens the soul into an instrument to improve the world. The Theosophist says, 'I accept', or 'I resign'. The Christian says. 'I resist'.

The fundamental difference in outlook is due to a basic difference in the conception of God. The Theosophist's God is impersonal justice. The Christian's God co-operates with man to make all things work together for good.

In addition, Theosophy falls under censure for its inherent contradiction. For, while it urges that God is impersonal, the 'superconsciousness', the Deity is given such personal attributes as 'loving', 'just', and 'truthful'.

Furthermore, the christology of the Theosophists is seriously defective and arbitrarily unhistorical. Mrs Besant has had the effrontery to produce her own gospel. According to her, Jesus was born a hundred years before his presumed nativity, was trained in a desert community of the Essenes, where he learned the esoteric wisdom of the East from visiting Indian and Egyptian sages. She further maintains that the 'Christ' part of his nature was added at baptism but withdrawn during the crucifixion and that he returned to teach his disciples the mysteries for a period of fifty years. She equates Jesus with Buddha and Confucius as one of the masters of the spiritual life. Christian orthodoxy cannot accept this caricature of the founder of the faith.

The teaching about man and salvation. The Theosophists have a very peculiar doctrine concerning man. They assert that each individual is compounded of seven parts. The most common classification is the following: the physical body, the etheric double (or vital body), the astral (or emotional) body, the mental body, the causal body, the future body, the perfected body. Salvation consists in moving from body to body until perfection is reached in the seventh body. Successively, the unimportant parts of the self are sloughed off like the unwanted skins of a snake. Or, in the biting words of Father Bede Frost, this is 'the strip-tease of the soul'.

What is to be thought of this teaching concerning the seven parts or bodies of man? To say the least of it, it is very muddled psychology. Man cannot be divided into physical, vital, emotional, mental and volitional parts and retain the unity of his personality. All these faculties of man are employed simultaneously, not successively. A simple instance may be taken – that of a footballer scoring a goal. The kick is physical, the placing of the kick is mental, the fact that the toe connects with the ball is vital, the will to kick is volitional and the joy that a good kick brings is emotional; these are all parts of one simultaneous reaction and action. They are only divisible on reflection, not in action. Indeed, if they took place successively, it is doubtful if any footballer would ever score a goal! Human personality cannot be divided into five parts, let alone seven. As for the future body or the perfect body, there seems to be no relation between them and the present personality of man. This psychology is confused because it isolates parts of human life that co-exist and refuse to be parted in the actual texture of experience.

But an even more serious criticism must be offered of the salvation envisaged by the Theosophists. It consists in killing the body that the soul may live. But the body is not evil, it is the instrument of the soul. It is the medium through which the soul communicates with the outer world and with other souls. What alone is evil is the abuse of the body.

Theosophists make the mistake of saying, 'Get rid of the body and you get rid of evil'. But, as Jesus reminded his disciples, it is evil thoughts that corrupt, not the body. Salvation must be wrought in the inner citadel of the mind and imagination; therefore there is no real salvation to be found in mortifying the body, which is only the agent of evil thoughts and imaginings. Evil is not like a stain on the polished table that soils the surface; it is far more akin to dry rot that weakens and then destroys the interior of the wood. Humanity needs a new inner constitution, but the Theosophists offer us only French polishing. Our need is not evolution, but revolution.

The teaching about reincarnation. This is the most distinctive and important Theosophical tenet. It is this aspect of Theosophy which has attracted several men of distinction in the Western world, including Aldous Huxley and J. B. Priestley. In fact, the fine series of 'time-plays' written by Priestley have this as their central theme.

Like Christians, Theosophists have to unravel the age-old problem of the suffering of the innocent. How can they reconcile this with the belief in a wise and benevolent God? The Christian admits the difficulty. His tentative answer is that since we are bound together as families and nations the innocent must suffer with the guilty, for that is the price to be paid for human fellowship. Moreover, since God suffers in the affliction of his people this tragic experience can be transmuted to gain where it is accepted in faith, for suffering then becomes an impetus to Christian love.

Theosophy takes an easier path. It denies that there is any problem, since it denies that there are any innocent persons. We are all supposed to be suffering for sins committed in previous existences or reaping the advantages of previous virtues. We therefore deserve the penalties or rewards dealt out to us in this life. Thus if we are born diseased or defective, or in the midst of crime or poverty, it in the recompense of our former evil deeds; if we have noble dispositions, great abilities, or high positions, these were won by our own former merits. This is undeniably an attractive belief, because it reconciles the suffering in the world with the justice of God.

Its fundamental weakness lies in its failure to explain how suffering does benefit us. If I was a murderer in my last life and I am born deformed in this life, it is a judgment that I deserve. But, since I cannot recall the circumstances under which I was prompted to commit murder, how can such a judgment teach me repentance? How can I repent sins whose origin and nature I have forgotten? Since I cannot feel sorry, how can I improve? Moreover, if I am born deformed, I have no information to assure me that it was a just punishment. Is there more reason why I should say, 'I deserve it', than that I should curse the universe for my misfortune? These are some of the obstinate questions the doctrine of reincarnation provokes in Christian minds.

Furthermore, Theosophy, while professing to explain the inequalities of life, succeeds only in making them disappear in the mists of the past. We are then forced to ask, What caused the first unequal conditions or the first unequal actions?

Possibly the worst feature of the doctrine of reincarnation is that it paralyses the desire to improve the social environment and produces an ignoble fatalism. Since action is the fruit of desire, and desire must be abandoned, action is prohibited.

Moreover, it is no palliation to be told that things will be better in another existence. We wish to make the best of this life here and now. This belief in an impersonal justice has no dynamic in it. It is a conservatism of the soul, a religion of long-deferred hope.

Even the future life posited by Theosophy is only a pale shadow of the Christian doctrine of eternal life, not only because its realization may be almost indefinitely postponed, but also because it offers absorption or annihilation of individuality in the Infinite as its goal. The Christian doctrine of the perfection of the self is its complete contrary.

III

The chief criticism of Theosophy is that it appeals to the self-regarding motives. Its advice is, 'Make it easier for yourself in the next life.' This plea must be rejected by the Christian because he is not concerned primarily for a more comfortable existence in another world for himself; he wants a finer existence for his brethren in this world. He desires to be a reformer, not a pensioner. He cannot worship a God who is impartial justice. How can the thought of a divine pair of scales either inspire or comfort him? He needs a God who bleeds with humanity in its wounds and scars. He wants a God who will redeem society and remake man in his own image. He requires a saviour and a friend. He therefore turns to God's eternal and beloved Son, the carpenter of Nazareth, whose hands are blunted in life's workshop, the loving teacher and companion of the common people. He turns to the lonely crucified Son of God on the stark hill-top, who took his station among thieves.

The God of the Theosophists is too highbrow for the Christian. Their God is no more interested in our human struggle than a sleeping and gigantic elephant. The God of the Theosophists is busied with his mathematical calculations, apportioning exact retribution to our sins in different existences. His Impersonal Highness is, in short, merely a celestial calculating machine.

Christians cannot be persuaded to leave the God who met them in Christ Jesus and, without any assurance save their need, embraced them in the arms outspread on the jagged tree of Calvary. They stake their life on the fact that this God cares, because he treats our erring humanity so patiently; because, also, 'he gave his only-begotten Son that whosoever believeth on him should not perish but have everlasting life'. Christ is the proof that God cares. In him God gave us his word.

IV

The grandeur of the Christian faith is seen in comparison with the deficiencies in Theosophy which it can supply. Christianity offers us a true view of sin. For the Theosophist a sense of personal sin is thought of as weak and degrading. Forgiveness, too, is inadmissible for the Theosophist because it would represent a diminution of strict justice. No new start is possible for the Theosophist in this life, but only in the next, and a man must work out his own slow salvation without the assistance of God.

There is no redemption from the power of evil in Theosophy, either. The World Teachers or Bodhisattvas of Theosophy offer teaching and enlightenment and, occasionally, example. But human nature needs more – it requires the infusion of new life. It is only Jesus Christ who said, 'I am come that they might have life and have it more abundantly.'

Theosophy knows little of the meaning of sacrifice, which includes vicarious suffering. Their ideal man practises detachment to kill desire. But this is a striking contrast to the Saviour, who 'though he was a Son, yet learned obedience through the things which he suffered', who 'was in all points tempted like as we are, yet without sin', who, as the sinless penitent, 'hath borne our griefs and carried our sorrows'.

Because of Christ's coming to serve the world, Christians cannot be content with their own salvation. They can rest only when the kingdoms of this world become kingdoms of our God and of his Christ. There is only one faith to live by: the faith of the apostles, enshrined in the creed of that name. This has been admirably summed up by Dr Norman Macleod thus: 'There is a Father in Heaven who loves us, a Brother who died for us, and a Spirit who helps us to be good, and a Home where we shall all meet at the last.' That is a creed that will see humanity through this life into the next. It is, if need be, a creed to die for; it is assuredly a creed to live for.

NOTES

1. James Black, *New Forms of the Old Faith,* Nelson, London 1948, p.58.

FURTHER READING

The chief original sources of the cult are Helena Blavatsky's *Isis Unveiled* and *The Secret Doctrine*, published by the Theosophical University Press. The writings of Annie Besant and Charles W. Leadbeater are also important, especially the latter's *Outline to Theosophy* and *Textbook of Theosophy*. These are all issued by the Theosophical Publishing House.

Farquhar, J. N., *Modern Religious Movements in India*, Macmillan, London and New York 1918.

Kuhn, Alvin B., *Theosophy, a Modern Revival of Ancient Wisdom,* Henry Holt, New York 1930.

Ransom, Josephine, *A Short History of the Theosophical Society*, Theosophical Publishing House 1938.

Ryan, Charles James, *What is Theosophy?*, Covina, 2nd ed., California 1944.

11 Scientology

*Now all the Athenians and the strangers
sojourning there spent their time in
nothing else but either to tell or hear
some new thing* (Acts 17.21)

Although religion is a matter of faith, and science is concerned with matters of fact, in sceptical days particular religions have claimed to be scientific. One example, as its name implies, is Christian Science, the therapeutic theology of Mary Baker Eddy. Another example is Scientology, which its most recent interpreter, George Malko, calls in the title of his book *Scientology: the Now Religion.*[1]

The intention, of course, is to claim that here is a proven and practical philosophy of life which is of universal relevance, and that will commend itself to intelligent men and women who might otherwise repudiate religion as mere superstition. Thus the name of 'the Church of Scientology' has a magnetic and attractive advertising value. In June 1955, the 'Founding Church of Scientology' was established in Washington, DC.

It is, as a matter of fact, an open question whether Scientology is a religion, and it is even more questionable whether it is a 'church'. It claims to be a church and to have 15,000,000 members. It has ministers who wear clerical collars and vestments. Until a recent challenge it had tax-exempt status as a recognized religion in the United States. Yet it is exceedingly dubious whether it is a church, since it makes no claim to be founded on the life, work, or teaching of Jesus Christ of Nazareth, as all other churches do, though some may add scriptures other than those of the Old and New Testaments (like the Mormons).

Most religions demand a belief in God or gods, though Confucianism represents a religion that is ethical rather than theological. Even so, they believe that the values which they enshrine are the ultimate constituents of reality. While it could be argued that later developments of Scientology have vague ideas about 'spirituality', there is no sense in which Scientology can be said to serve the will of God or to create men and women of integrity.

What, then, is Scientology?

I

It has been called a 'subtle union of *The Power of Positive Thinking*, a Dale Carnegie course, some kind of self-hypnosis, and a liberal spicing of the most refined science-fiction'.[2] This may be clarified, at least in part, by the declaration of aim offered by Robert Thomas, the director of Scientology in the United States. The latter affirmed: 'What we're really trying to do is increase a person's confidence in being able to remember what he wants to remember, and not remember what he doesn't want to remember, and to increase his confidence by being able to control his memories.' Scientology, then, is a type of thought-technique aimed at maximizing confidence in one's self. What inspires so many of the pupils of its inventor, L. Ron Hubbard, is his assurance to them that not only can they not fail to improve the working of their minds, but they can ultimately make them into perfect thinking machines. Such a promise not only gives assurance to the recipient, but, like ancient Gnosticism, flatters him that he is one of the most intelligent initiates in the world. These convictions are reinforced by a whole series of courses, each of a higher standard of requirement, which the keen scientologist undertakes (and the tests which prove his mastery). Even the high costs of these courses in mental control reassure the takers of their great value to personality development. (But, incidentally, it is the profits accruing to the founder of Scientology which have convinced the US internal revenue service and the courts that Scientology is neither a religious nor a non-profit foundation.)

II

Who is Lafayette Ronald Hubbard, the founder of Scientology? To Scientologists he is, of course, *the* father figure whose voice they hear on endless tapes of his lectures, or the wise, practical and imaginative sage whose prolific books and pamphlets they are required to read to keep in good standing with the Church of Scientology. They may even have seen him lecture, though this is less likely than ever in recent years since he appears to have lived in isolation on a converted cattleboat on the Mediterranean after his headquarters at East Grinstead in Sussex, England, were closed down. When he was visible to his disciples, he was seen as a confident, candid, natural, and jovial man of great conviction and warmth.

He was born in 1911 in Tilden, Nebraska, one of the chief Western states devoted chiefly to cattle-raising. His father was a commander in the United States Navy. This accounts for the boy spending his earliest years on a Montana cattle-ranch owned by his maternal grandmother.

At twelve he went to live in the capital, Washington, where his father was stationed, and two years later he went to China with his father. He has travelled widely. At the age of nineteen he entered George Washington University. He commenced training as a civil engineer, but it seems that he did not complete the training. The doctorate that has occasionally appeared after his name was granted by Sequoia University of California, an institution not widely known or academically highly evaluated. He seems to have either led or been a member of four expeditions organized to study primitive peoples. When not engaged in anthropoligical exploration, he devoted his time to writing science fiction for such popular magazines as *Astounding Science Fiction* and *Thrilling Wonder Stories*. In World War II he was an officer in the United States Navy, commissioned in the Philippines before Pearl Harbor. The official biography authorized by Scientology affirms that Hubbard was flown home in the late spring of 1942 as 'the first returned US casualty from the Far East'.

The first proof of his interest in improving the powers of the human mind was the publication of the earlier prototype of Scientology known as 'Dianetics'. This book bore the full title of *Dianetics: the Modern Science of Mental Health.* Such a title seemed to suggest that Jules Verne had rewritten the text book of Mary Baker Eddy. Hubbard was not bashful in his claim for the new psychological technique he was propagating. The opening sentence of the book indicated that humility was regarded as a weakness by the founder of the new religion. It read thus: 'The creation of dianetics is a milestone for man comparable to his discovery of fire and superior to his inventions of the wheel and the arch.'

Hubbard drew a distinction between the *analytical* mind that perceives, remembers and reasons, and the *reactive.* mind (corresponding to Freud's unconscious) which only records. The analytic mind is normally in control of the reactive mind, except when injury, anaesthesia or a traumatic shock or pain causes the analytic mind to switch off. In such an emergency situation the reactive mind produces 'engrams' or complete impressions. Dianetics is the method for pulling these 'engrams' from the reactive mind in order to study them with a view to getting rid of such supposedly crippling memories. Probing to dredge up an 'engram' is known as 'auditing'. After about twenty hours of 'auditing' a person is qualified as a 'release'. The next stage is when the same person becomes a 'preclear' and, finally, a 'clear' – that is, absolutely clear or free of 'engrams'.

III

Scientology is a further development of Dianetics in both theory and practice. The human spirit is now named *theta* – the personality separable from the body and mind without causing mental derangement or death. Scientology became the technique of attaining the enlightened discovery of one's own *theta*, which replaced the older notion of 'clear'.

In 1954 a new instrument was invented, supposedly to make auditing more exact. It was known as an 'Electropsychometer' or 'E-Meter'. It was supposed to register degrees of stress from moment to moment. Hubbard has said that to audit without an E-Meter is like hunting ducks at midnight by firing in all directions.

Scientology teaches that there are 'eight dynamics of existence'. These are areas in which the fully developed mind must feel at home. The first is the self-dynamic. The second dynamic is the sexual. The third dynamic is the group dynamic. The fourth is mankind. The fifth is the animal dynamic. The sixth is the dynamic of the universe (composed of Matter, Energy, Space and Time, or M-E-S-T). The seventh is the spiritual dynamic (or the urge towards existence as or of spirits). The eighth or final dynamic is the infinity or God dynamic. The full life is one which expresses these urges towards participation in and knowledge of these dynamics or modes or aspects of existence.

The importance of the method of Scientology is that it enables its adherents to advance to greater mental control. This is, in fact, tested on what is termed a 'tone scale'. At the positive top of the scale is serenity at 40, and below it the following gradations: 8.0 exhilaration; 4.0 enthusiasm; 3.0 conservatism; 2.5 boredom; 2.0

antagonism; 1.8 pain; 1.5 anger; 1.2 no sympathy; 1.1 covert hostility; 1.0 fear; down to 0 being a body (death) and a failure. The negative scale goes from −0.2 being other bodies (explained as regret) to −8.0 which equals hiding.

The aim of Scientology is to raise the individual in the tone scale so as to improve his or her abilities and to rehabilitate the *theta* by removing aberrations. This is of prime urgency, because if completed during this lifetime, all future lives of the *thetan* will be problem-free.

Other conceptions, concerning the previous histories of *thetans* in aeons of time, their implantation at implant stations, and their journeys through the further recesses of space, are so speculative and putative as to be mind-boggling. In the nature of things they can neither be affirmed nor denied; so they may as well be disregarded.

The process of maturing through the various grades, assuming the learner is successful, is a costly and arduous one. The cost is approximately $4,028 (or over £1,600 sterling) to go through all the grades of Scientology. Grades O to IV are the first grades of release (costing $750). Next follows the Dianetics auditor's course (cost $500). Then the scientologist advances to the power grade V—VA (costing $775). Grade VI is the solo grade, because it is done alone, without an instructor (cost $775). The final grade, VII, leads to being a 'clear' (cost $800).

IV

Hubbard's history is one of failure followed by heroic new starts. First the Dianetic Research Foundation was established in 1950, but by 1952 Hubbard had to file a petition for bankruptcy. Like the fabled phoenix, however, Hubbard's new projects rose from the ashes of the old.

Next it was the turn of Scientology. In June 1955 the Founding Church of Scientology was established in Washington DC, and incorporated in New York in November of the same year. By 1959 Saint Hill, near East Grinstead in Sussex, was established as the world headquarters of Scientology. Yet by 1963 the US government was filing a suit demanding 'seizure or condemnation' of the E-Meter as a fraudulent medical device, and by 1966 the US internal revenue service was investigating the tax-exempt and religious status of the Founding Church of Scientology. They were dubious about a religious enterprise making so much profit, especially when they found that in Washington DC alone the Founding Church took in $756,962 and that ninety per cent of this money came from fees and not donations. To add to Ron Hubbard's dismay, in 1968 the British Government prevented non-English nationals from entering Britain solely to study or practise Scientology. Earlier still Victoria, a state of the Commonwealth of Australia, had appointed a board of inquiry to investigate the claims of Scientology. This, after sitting for 160 days, hearing 151 witnesses and taking 8,920 pages of evidence, concluded in its report of 1965: 'However Hubbard may appear to his followers, the board can form no other view than that Hubbard is a fraud and scientology is fraudulent.'[3]

V

How is this technique of personality health and mental improvement to be evaluated?

First, it is exceedingly doubtful whether this new movement is religious in any generally accepted sense of that adjective, despite its quasi-religious vocabulary. It has no theology worthy of the name, and its use of such terms as 'spiritual' and 'infinity' as equal to 'God' and 'church' without reference to Jesus the founder of the church, seems to be a verbal camouflage to escape taxation rather than being integral to the philosophy of the movement, in which they play virtually no part.

Secondly, the movement is so clearly aimed at the improvement of the acuity of the mind of the individual (without any concern for others) that it is devoid of ethical teaching. Indeed, negatively speaking, it is concerned only for its own survival value. Furthermore, the ruthless suppression of the ideas of anyone trying to improve on the system makes it suspicious even as a philosophy supposedly in search of truth.

Thirdly, this suspicion is heightened by the methods of advertising and recruiting Scientology has employed. Two such methods deserve careful consideration. One was the so-called 'illness researches'. This required advertisements to be placed in newspapers with the aim of hunting out the victims of certain serious illnesses, claiming that a research foundation wished to interview the sufferers. When contact was established, the victims would be audited by a scientologist and were urgently recommended to join the Founding Church of Scientology. Even more grisly was another method of recruiting members, known as the 'casualty contact'.

The local contact was requested to scan local newspapers for the names (and, if possible, the addresses) of bereaved or injured persons, to call on the families of such, and to leave a visiting card listing the address of the Scientology church and days and hours of its services, which were said to be free. This mode of recruitment is nothing less than ghoulish, since it exploits people when they are at their weakest and most vulnerable. It is believed that they have been discontinued. But why were they ever started?

Fourthly, even in terms of the psychological aims of the movement (apart altogether from the religious question), Scientology can be seriously faulted. Instead of liberating persons, it seems to make them more subservient to a system, discourages the art of self-criticism and almost turns its devotees into automata.

Fifthly, there is so much sheer fantasy masquerading as philosophy in the system of Scientology that it can hardly be said to provide a solid and rational basis for life.

Then it may be asked: how do you account for the attraction of Scientology? In part, its appeal is to the ambitious and to those who – at the opposite end of the scale – are conscious of being drifters, and of living without a purpose in a relativistic and even nihilistic world. It provides a purpose for existence. It also provides a profound sense of togetherness for those who belong to the movement. Moreover, it is able to quantify the assessment of the tone qualities of the personality to which it aspires. In this and other ways a supposed science purporting to be a religion appears to offer the advantages of two worlds: this one and the next. And its founder is a man of great imaginative inventiveness, cordiality and enthusiasm.

NOTES

1. George Malko, *Scientology: the Now Religion*, New York 1970.
2. Malko, op. cit., p.6.
3. Ibid., p.80, where the conclusion of the report is cited.

FURTHER READING

Various publications of the Hubbard Association of Scientologists International, especially the textbooks and lectures of L. Ron Hubbard and the Professional Auditors' Bulletin.
Malko, George, *Scientology: the Now Religion*, New York 1970.

12 A Survey

*Jesus said, 'I am the way, the truth, and
the life; no one cometh unto the Father
but by me.'* (John 14.6)

From the first day of the Christian church, Christians have had
to fight the battle of faith on two fronts: spiritual and intellectual.
While the martyrs outlived and outdied their opponents, the apolo-
gists out-thought them.

The task of apologetics, the intellectual defence of the Christian
faith, changes from age to age, as new opponents arise to challenge
Christian doctrine. None the less, throughout church history the
systems that rival Christianity appear to fall into four main classes:
(1) the denial of spiritual values and of the existence of God, which
may be termed atheism on its intellectual side, and materialism or
secularism on its cultural and social side; (2) the claims to finality
made by religions other than Christianity; (3) a Judaistic perver-
sion of the Christian faith; (4) a Gnostic eclecticism, an anthology
of Christian and non-Christian beliefs. Our concern is exclusively
with the perversions and distortions of Christianity such as are
included within the third and fourth categories.

I

The first council of the Christian church in Jerusalem had to face
the living issue: how much Judaism shall non-Jewish converts to
the Christian faith be expected to embrace? Was the Law valid now
that Christians lived under the sphere of grace? Judaistic Christianity has sometimes been described as the retention of the scaffold-
ing even when the headstone of the corner has been placed in
position: that is, an attempt to gain salvation by obedience to the
prescriptions of the Jewish Law, instead of a life of trust in the

merits and mediation of Jesus Christ in the strength of the Holy Spirit. Many Christians in all centuries have found it difficult to accept the ethical imperative of love. They would prefer to regard their religion as the observance of a code of prohibitions, rather than believe, with St Augustine of Hippo, that the Christian has only one relevant injunction, 'love God and do what you like'. The ethic of the second mile is both more exacting and more exhilarating, and it does not appeal to cautious souls. Thus, from the earliest days, legalism has always fought against the life of the Spirit. The other persistently-recurring element of Judaism within Christianity has been millenarianism, and, moreover, one more material than spiritual in its allocation of rewards to the faithful.

Judaistic tendencies show themselves in the following 'Christian' movements: Seventh-Day Adventism, Jehovah's Witnesses, British-Israel and Mormonism. Seventh-Day Adventism revives sabbatarianism, making it a doctrine essential for salvation, and in its millenarianism limits the number of the elect to its own members. The Jehovah's Witnesses develop their doctrine of soul-sleep and their millenarianism on an Old Testament foundation. They also circumscribe salvation by limiting it to their own communion. The British-Israelites have reduced the doctrine of election to favouritism and their God to an Anglo-Saxon tribal deity. The patriarchial ethics and the apocalypticism of Mormonism reflect a Judaistic, rather than a Christian, colouring. The success of these Judaistic revisions of Christianity forces on Christians the question : What home truths have these sects to teach the churches? These lessons appear to be three. Firstly, their adherents have a knowledge of the contents of the Holy Scriptures which Christians would do well to emulate. The Bible is the record of the revelation of the mighty acts of God consummated in the life, death, resurrection and ascension of Jesus Christ, and the donation of the Holy Spirit; it is the supreme witness to the origin of our faith, and trust in Christ as the contemporary Lord recreated and nourished by it. For this reason alone it is imperative that Christians should become again the people of the Book. The very facility with which adherents of Judaistic sects cite chapter and verse of the scriptures and the enthusiasm with which Communists con their 'Red Bible', *Das Kapital* of Karl Marx, should drive Christians back to the word as their iron-rations and marching orders.

But that is not enough, for clearly a thorough knowledge of the Bible has not prevented the new movements from being heretical. In the second place, what is required is a *critical* knowledge of the

Holy Writ. Biblicism becomes heretical because it has no standard of reference by which to evaluate the different parts of the scriptures. Claiming to believe that the Bible is equally inspired in all its parts, it nevertheless builds on private interpretation of a selection of the Law and of the apocalyptic parts of scripture. The only adequate criterion is 'the mind of Christ' by which Christians understand the life of our Lord as recorded in those superb biographies, the Gospels, and in the leading of the Holy Spirit given to the apostles and recorded in the other books of the New Testament. This standard disenthralls the Christian from the authority of the old dispensation and translates him 'into the kingdom of the love of God's dear Son'. For 'the Law came by Moses, but grace and truth by Christ'. His ethical motivation is the constraint of the love of Christ. The morality of justice under the old dispensation is replaced by the profounder understanding of forgiveness which is, according to Dr Reinhold Niebuhr, 'the crown of Christian ethics'. Whatever in the old covenant is contrary to the attitude or the acts of Christ is un-Christian or sub-Christian, and therefore of no authority for the Christian man. In particular, a critical understanding of the scriptures liberates the Christian from regarding prophetical and apocalyptic books as cryptograms from which the ingenious bibliolater may predict the future in detail.

The success of these movements should, in fact, force the Christian church to attempt a thorough revaluation not only of the Bible, but of the Holy Spirit and of the church itself as the source of authority for Christian doctrine. History has shown that the Bible of itself, when regarded as infallible and equally inspired in all its parts, leads to the formation of heretical sects. It also shows that an exclusive dependence upon the Holy Spirit leads to such aberrations as characterized the fantastic 'rule of the saints' in the days of the Commonwealth in England, when every man claimed his idiosyncracies as new revelations; and that exclusive dependence upon the church as the organ of truth leads to the propounding of unbiblical doctrines, such as the Assumption of the Blessed Virgin and the Immaculate Conception, as of the essence of the faith. The Bible, the church and the individual inspired by the Holy Spirit are three interlocking authorities for the Christian faith. It is clear that the Bible is of primary, the church of secondary and the inspired individual of tertiary importance. The new movements have at least helped the church to reconsider the problem of authority. The groups may be thanked for this at least, that they are forcing the contemporary church to realize its urgency.

In the third place, the 'Judaistic' heretics have an enthusiasm in communicating their erratic tenets which Christians would do well to emulate in the spreading of the truth as it is in Christ Jesus. As instances of this we may take the remarkable organization of the Jehovah's Witnesses which obliges each of their members to canvass every householder in the interests of their doctrines, so much so that they have become a by-word for importunity and pertinacity, and the missionary zeal of the Seventh-Day Adventists and Mormons who have a reputation second only to the Moravians for the high proportion of their adherents who become missionaries in all parts of the earth. The warning of Professor J. R. Coates is timely:

> The success of heresies and unorthodox cults is a measure of the failure of the Church. As with Spiritualism, Christian Science, and Adventism, so with British-Israel: its propagandists minister to real human needs, and its plausibility is largely due to its ingenuity in relating the Bible to contemporary experience and to current affairs.[1]

II

Several other cults brought under review belong to the Gnostic type of heresy. They represent attempts to combine elements of Christian teaching with doctrines of other systems or faiths. The early Christians had to counter not only a Judaizing tendency but also a Hellenistic movement. Dr Radford rightly explains the attractions of such eclecticism as due

> partly to the desire to combine non-Christian ideas with Christian ideas, or to winning outsiders by going as near as possible to their position, and in still larger part to the wish of thinking men to understand and explain the Christian faith for thinking men.[2]

Many philosophers have attempted to find a common religion which summed up the spiritual values of all religions from the days of Lord Herbert of Cherbury to our contemporary, Professor Hocking of Harvard. To them doctrine was the ineffectual attempt of the different religions to capture in words the ineffable experiences of the mystics and the moralists. They argued that it ought to be possible to express the same experiences in common concepts. The renewed impetus to provide a common religion for humanity derives partly from the comparative study of religion, partly from the conviction that it is better for an increasingly secular civilization to have one religion than none, and partly from a desire to end nationalism and internecine warfare by acknowledging an overarching loyalty to one authoritative creed. Whilst several religions have been considered for the honour of being acclaimed the universal religion of mankind, the Christian faith has been found wanting by philosophers both because of its claim for finality and for its 'scandal of particularity'. Christians have stubbornly refused to allow their Saviour to consort on terms of equality in their estimation with Confucius, the Buddha, or Mohammed, the 'seal of the prophets'. Thus their claim that the Incarnation of the eternal Son of God is the final revelation of the nature and activity of God makes them unable to relegate the Christ to a convenient pantheon in which all religious teachers are worshipped alike. The anchor of their faith in history, as recorded in the saga of the mighty acts of God, means that Christianity cannot be reduced to a philosophy.

Examples of the Gnostic type of heresy are Theosophy, Scientology, Spiritualism and Christian Science. Its adherents are often former Christians. Of contemporary Gnosticism, Dr Radford says:

> The creed by which the Christian Scientist explains the facts of faith-healing is a latter-day Gnosticism which denies not merely the spiritual possibilities of the material world but also its reality as an object of experience. Theosophy is a latter-day Gnosticism which dissolves the Gospel into an allegory, fills the spiritual world with the creations of Hindu fancy, and now is summoning Christendom and all other religions to look to the East for another reincarnation of the Christ-spirit as the world teacher who is to inaugurate a new world-faith.[3]

We may note that Gnostic eclecticisms have the following features in common. Their religion appeals to the proud rather than the humble in heart, for it claims to sum up the best in other religions and thus castigates adherents of the older faiths as old-fashioned. The appeal is largely to intellectuals and initiates and not to the great under-privileged multitudes of the world. Their philosophy is almost always pantheistic and shares the characteristic weakness of that outlook; for example, it despises the body which for the Christian is the temple of the Holy Spirit; it teaches an automatic immortality which makes an end of a moral interpretation of history; it depersonalizes God so that he becomes an 'essence' or a 'principle' and ceases to be *the* Person; consequently it despises history and the world as illusory, and shows an ostrich-like optimism towards sin, and an unwillingness to change the social conditions, which militate against the full development of personality-in-community. Salvation is through identification with God by means of mediation, not by the transformation of the will.

The criticism of any attempt to find a common religion such as Theosophy is that no religion can be successful which builds only upon the highest common factors in all religions. The history of eighteenth-century Deism in England, with its attempt to banish distinctive doctrines in the interests of a religion that could be accepted by all men of good sense, proves that the resulting creed was ineffectual in the attempt to transform the lives of men. John Howe rightly parodied it as affirming, 'There shall be a God, provided he be not meddlesome.' Furthermore, the different religions do not mix, because they teach different, not common, tenets. Christianity is both world-affirming and world-denying. Buddhism is entirely world-denying. Christianity affirms that God the father is Creator and Controller of the universe. Buddhism denies the existence of a personal God at all. Yet it is mainly these two religions which Theosophy has tried to combine.

The mistake of Spiritualism and Christian Science, which have closer affinities with the Christian faith, is to attempt to make one Christian tenet into the whole of Christianity. Although Professor Bethune-Baker was writing of early heresiarchs, his explanation of the motivation of heresy is applicable to both Spiritualism and Christian Science. He declares that heterodoxy arose

> when they seized on a few facts as though they were all the facts, and from these few framed theories to explain and interpret all; when they put forward a meagre and immature conception as a full-grown representation of the Christian idea of life.[4]

In each case the success of these two cults has been due to the failure of the church to keep in the forefront of its teaching the truths which they seceded to maintain. The Spiritualists have re-affirmed the centrality of the doctrine of the Resurrection in the Christian faith, and have taken the belief in the communion of saints as the centre and sum of their faith. The Christian Scientists have seen the overwhelming importance of faith in the New Testament narratives and applied it to the sicknesses of humanity. In fact, both the doctrine of the communion of saints and the practice of faith-healing are important constituents of the Christian faith and life. These needed to be reaffirmed, but the mistake of the heretics was to assert that they comprehended the entire faith.

It has been already remarked that Gnostic heresies find the readiest converts amongst weak Christians. This provides an obvious lesson for the historic churches. Their candidates for confirmation or membership must be instructed in the biblical faith as summarized in the Apostles' Creed, in Christian conduct as summarized in the Decalogue and the Beatitudes, and in Christian devotions as summarized in the Lord's Prayer. A thorough understanding of these is a minimal necessity for every Christian.

A fascinating factor in modern heresies which deserves the attention of the churches is the important part played by women in their foundation and continuance. It is surely significant that the two founders of Theosophy were Madame Blavatsky and Mrs Annie Besant, that Christian Science owes its origin to Mrs Mary Baker Eddy, and that the originator of Seventh-Day Adventism was Mrs Ellen White. It might be suggested that in each case men had pioneered the thought-forms of the new systems, but none the less the success of these cults is due to the drive of energetic women. Can this fact have any significance for the churches? One reason for the interest of women in these new faiths is that their place is recognized in their hierarchies, as it is not in the historic Christian churches. Although Christians have affirmed for almost twenty centuries with St Paul that 'there is neither male nor female, but all are one in Christ Jesus', this belief rarely results in the ordination of women, far less in their elevation to a high place in the government of the Christian church. Only a small number of women ministers exist in the Protestant churches; as yet the Roman Catholic and Orthodox churches do not admit women to the priesthood. The Society of Friends does not ordain either men or women, but both sexes have equal rights and privileges. If all the churches were to remove this form of sexual discrimination, the temptation for devout women to set up their own forms of cults, or to gravitate towards those sects that accord women a higher status, would be greatly reduced. Furthermore, it seems that the heretical cults founded by women show a warmth of fellowship that is so often unwarrantably absent in the historic churches. The same warmth partly accounts for the success of the Moral Re-Armament movement.

III

Is it possible to catalogue the tendencies of the new movements in such a way as to underline their strength and weakness? The attempt will be made to summarize those factors which two or three of them hold in common. These may serve as useful danger signals to the members of both the new movements and the historic churches.

There is the danger of mistaking the part for the whole in Christian faith or practice. Two examples are Christian Science and Theosophy.

There is the danger of an over-emphasis on the Old Testament to the detriment of the New. Examples of this tendency are Jehovah's Witnesses, Seventh-Day Adventism, Mormonism and British-Israel.

There is the danger of confusing Christianity with Pantheism. Both Theosophy and Christian Science are examples of this confusion.

There is the danger of seeking for greater assurance in the religious life than faith in Christ offers. Spiritualism, with its attempt to obtain experimental proof of life after death, is one example, and the predictions of the millenarian groups provide another. Each is a product of scepticism rather than of trust.

There is the danger of spiritual pride which issues in the schism of a 'holier-than-thou' attitude, or in the formation of an esoteric cult for initiates or intellectuals only. Diverse examples of this characteristic are found in Moral Re-Armament, Theosophy and some of the millenarian groups. The corrective is the charity of the one holy catholic and apostolic church, of which the historic communions are branches, honouring individuals of all races and classes and types.

There is the danger of using God as a means to an end. This is the case when God is a convenience for obtaining excellent health in Christian Science, or as a means of obtaining political leadership in the world as in British-Israel, or as the supreme weapon in defeating Communism as conceived by the MRA, or as the goal for Scientology of mind improvement.

There is the danger of individualistic pietism, quietism and a concentration on 'glory for me'. Its correlative is the renunciation of many civic and political responsibilities, and is evinced by Theosophists, Jehovah's Witnesses, Christian Scientists and Seventh-Day Adventists. It also contributed to the success of Marxism by causing the latter to condemn Christianity as 'dope'.

There is the supreme danger of failing to acknowledge the fullness, the uniqueness and the finality of the Christian doctrine of the

Incarnation. Nearly all groups suffer from this defect, otherwise they would not have come into being. Where Jesus is thought of as a first-century teacher and inspired prophet, as was often the case in communions which accepted what was known as a 'reduced christology', the way was already open for the displacement of Jesus by later and self-appointed prophets like Ellen White, Mary Baker Eddy, Joseph Smith or Annie Besant. Where he is accepted as the eternal and only-begotten Son of God, and worshipped as the Lord of lords and King of kings, and obeyed as Master, Christian humility makes it unlikely for a mere human to pretend to a better insight into the mind of God than Jesus had.

IV

'Mainstream' Christianity will be most attractive when it is most true to its own inheritance. If it cares for the bodies, the souls and the organization of a just order of society, it will have nothing to fear from Communism. If the fellowship of Christians is a genuine community and family springing from their communion with the God and Father of us all, if Christian members confess their sins in sincerity and with a desire to make reparation to those whom they have wronged, and if they provide a way of life with opportunities of thrilling service for its younger members, historic Christianity can dispense with Moral Re-Armament services. If it places the doctrines of the Resurrection and of the communion of saints in the centre of its worship, the spurious attractions of Spiritualism will be unavailing because dispelled by faith in the Risen Christ. If Christianity takes seriously the miraculous powers of faith in a wonder-working God, Christian Science will lose its attractions. If Christians really believe that their Lord has won a triple victory over sin, suffering and death, and that 'all things work together for good to them that love God', they will not relapse into the superstition of astrology. If the churches proclaim of Christ by life and by lip that 'there is none other Name whereby we must be saved', Scientology and Theosophy will lose their enchantments. If the church by its abounding charity manifests in its international and interracial fellowship that there is neither 'Jew nor Greek, bond nor free', and that God is no respecter of persons, all racialistic distortions of the faith such as British-Israel will earn the unceasing antagonism of Christians. If Christians accept the general promises of Christ, and do not try to implement his reverent silences with details drawn from their own materialistic imaginations, and show a comparable zeal for transmitting their holy faith, then the unseemly predictions of the Seventh-Day Adventists and Jehovah's Witnesses will lose their interest.

In the last analysis, however, there must be a radical change in the approach of the historic churches to these new movements. Clarity must be supplemented with charity.

NOTES

1. *Expository Times*, Vol. LIV, p.313.

2. Lewis Radford, *Ancient Heresies in Modern Dress*, Robertson, Melbourne 1913, p.34.

3. Ibid, p.34.

4. *An Introduction to the Early History of Christian Doctrine*, Methuen, London 1938, pp.4f.

13 Epilogue: The Way of Encounter

Speaking the truth with love
(Ephesians 4.15)

However sympathetically we have tried to look at the new spiritual movements hitherto, we have necessarily observed them from the *outside*. In so doing, it is inevitable that we should have stressed the differences between them and the historic Christian churches. This Epilogue will emphasize the important possibilities latent in a more positive approch of personal and group encounter with a view to *inside* appreciation and understanding. The relations between Roman Catholics, Orthodox, Anglicans and Protestants are closer at present than they have ever been before. It is essential that there should be a determined attempt to draw together the historic Christian churches and the spiritual movements, especially those of a Christian intention among the latter. Taking the whole spectrum of movements discussed in this book, it is clear that encounter will be welcomed by some, unwelcome to others and probably a matter of sheer indifference to yet others.

In this situation it is important to try to do three things. First, we must attempt to discern those signs by which a movement is developing into a denomination, and particularly a denomination that seeks closer association with the historic Christian churches. For convenience, we shall describe the movement towards the centre of the historic churches as *centripetal*, and the movement away from the centre as *centrifugal*. We are, then, looking for signs of change from a centrifugal to a centripetal direction. Secondly, we must identify those movements which are clearly centripetal. Thirdly, by a new attitude on our part, and by actions clearly reflecting that attitude, we must encourage and accelerate the centripetal movement.

I

What signs mark the change in direction from hostility to growing appreciation of the historic churches on the part of new spiritual movements?

(1) *Social approximation.* Throughout these pages it has been urged that there are social as well as theological factors accounting for the original hostility and mutual suspicion. By the same token, when social differences between the older denominations and newer movements lessen, a mutual appreciation becomes possible. As we shall see later, it does not inevitably follow that social approximation leads to theological approximation, but it removes an important ground of misunderstanding.

In the increased prosperity of modern America, as in the British welfare state, there is a higher common level of education and a higher appreciation of culture. The 'disinherited' groups are coming into their inheritance. (And about time, too!) In consequence, 'side-stream' Christians increasingly wear clothes and use vocabularies indistinguishable from 'main-stream' Christians. 'Store-front' churches in the USA move into suburban areas and comply with the municipal building requirements. 'Tin tabernacles' in the UK yield to brick structures. Thus, apart from the names on the notice-boards, the churches of certain of the new movements are no different from the neo-Gothic of the Methodist church in the High Street or the neo-colonial United Church of Christ or the cantilevered sanctuaries of the new Roman Catholic or Episcopal churches on Main Street.

These Christians have arrived socially, and the older churches should hang out the flags, instead of muttering as they so often do. As long as the society is open-ended, even if the parents don't quite arrive, their children will. Thus, the social basis for suspicion is disintegrating.

This mixing process is speedier in America than in Britain, because of the great mobility of population in the States, where on an average one family in four changes its home each year. There are endless natural opportunities in parents'-and-teachers' associations, professional and trade gatherings and socials, and in factories, shops and offices. One hopes that unofficial dialogue will lead to official conversations.

(2) *The maturation of the second and third generation.* The enthusiasm of first-generation Bible-based movements is notoriously difficult to preserve in the second and third generations.

Success brings in numbers, and numbers require a complex organization. Inevitably the close-knit fellowship of the pioneers, despite the organization of gigantic conventions, leads to a remoteness from the grass roots. The increasingly complex organization at regional and national levels is further complicated by the need for specialists and institutions where evangelistic, social, educational and medical training may be provided. Relationships tend to become less spontaneous and more formal.

(3) As a result of the changes induced by the first and second factors, a third emerges. It is *the demand for a more educated ministry and a more predictable form of worship.*

Bible Institutes are admirable for training evangelists, but are not sophisticated enough for training ministers. Thus colleges and seminaries are founded. But if these institutions are to receive accreditation in the United States their teachers (at least a high proportion of them) must have doctoral degrees. Hence the reason for the most able and ambitious teachers and ministers attending the graduate schools of the large universities or university-related interdenominational seminaries, such as Harvard or Yale Divinity School or Union Seminary in New York City in the East, or Chicago Divinity School in the mid-West, or the Graduate Union of Seminaries at Berkeley in the far West.

The results can be imagined. In the free encounter such institutions provide, the representatives of the new movements contribute to the fracturing of stereotypes and prejudices. Personal friendships are made that cut across denominational frontiers. Many labels are found to be merely libels. An inevitable ecumenical chain-reaction ensues as a Presbyterian makes a life-long friend of a Pentecostalist or a Northern Baptist sees that a Seventh-Day Adventist is a comrade, not a competitor. All members of such an interdenominational seminary are responsible for conducting prayers, and there is at first hostility to and later a growing appreciation of the possibility of supplementing forms of prayer with free prayers, and a heightened appreciation of what the sacramental life means to Lutherans and Anglicans, for example. Slowly but surely, a more sophisticated theology emerges in the preaching and greater order and dignity in the conduct of divine worship.

(4) *Changes in theology and the Christian life.* The other changes we have marked also produce subtle transformations of emphasis in Christian belief and behaviour. Christianity is now recognized to be world-affirming as well as world-denying. As a result there is less emphasis on the immediacy of the Second Coming of Christ.

The hope is not denied; it is delayed. There is less interest in the possible predictions of the Apocalypse.

There are also likely to be changes in ethical patterns. These will probably include a deeper involvement in citizenship and community affairs, and a recognition that moral issues are rarely a choice between divine or diabolical alternatives. An original simplistic legalism will be transformed by the growing complexity of the involved life, by the need to make due allowances for different temperaments and circumstances, and, in short, the need to be more compassionate and less expulsive in church discipline.

(5) The most important sign of all is *an increase in charity to other religious groups.* (And who dares to say that the historic Christian churches are filled with charity and compassion?) This achievement (more properly an endowment) will be symbolized by the desire to issue – on the side of the older denominations – and to accept – on the side of the newer movements – invitations to join ministerial fraternals and the Evangelical Alliance. The centripetal movement will have gained great momentum when some of these movements have been welcomed into the comity of the World Council of Churches, the chief instrument and expression of ecumenism in the twentieth century.

II

Which of the new movements we have considered show these signs of centripetal movement, and which show the opposite centrifugal signs?

Of all the new movements the nearest to the historic Christian churches is that of the Jesus freaks, especially if the Catholic Pentecostalists are included as part of the Jesus movement. It could make the historic Christian churches jealous by its very dynamism, or it could all too easily become contemptuous of the static condition and cold impersonality of the Christian churches. It has not succumbed to either temptation. The historic churches, as was suggested earlier, should be both encouraging and wary in their relations with the Jesus freaks. They should encourage the fervour, the vigorous experimentation in approach, and the values of love and peace exemplified by Jesus and these, his newest disciples. But the historic Christian churches must remind the Jesus freaks that Christianity is a faith for foul weather and for the aged as well as for fair weather and the young. Moreover, they must be taught that a scriptural contextualism is necessary to offset their too great dependence upon proof-textualism and literalism in exegesis. This will, of course, require great openness and humility on the part of both parties, and a complete lack of dogmatism and authoritarianism on the side of the historic churches and of complacency on the side of the Jesus freaks, who should be taught to consider that we are not infallible, not even the youngest of us!

The centripetal movement is also shown, though to a lesser degree, by the Seventh-Day Adventists and associated groups. They, too, are a Christian missionary organization with international ramifications and unbounded zeal. They are engaged in medical, educational, social and evangelistic work that compels admiration. There is, however, still sufficient difference between them and the historic churches (in the observance of the seventh day and in their reinterpretation of the doctrine of the atonement) to put a brake on the predominantly centripetal movement.

Moral Re-Armament is both related to and independent from the historic churches. Many of its members are also members of the churches. Many others are not. For some it is a supplement to the work of the church; for others it is a moral and spiritual substitute for the church. It arose from the historic churches, Lutheran and Anglican. Conceivably, if it were so to choose, it might be reincorporated in the church. At present, however, it moves parallel to the church and is able to attract those who are beyond the immediate reach of the church. Its independence gives it great freedom for experimentation, but equally, as has been argued, it has lost some of the ballast and depth of tradition. Certainly it does not seem to be hostile to the historic churches, nor (however glad it is to get the support of individual churchmen) does it seem particularly friendly to denominations as denominations. It is an ideology and should not therefore be regarded as other than supplementing the ethical beliefs of Christianity. It could develop a centripetal movement.

The Mormons, or the Church of Jesus Christ of Latter-Day Saints, suggest a possibility of fruitful encounter with the 'mainstream' churches from their name, their missionary zeal and international extension, their social 'spread' and their acknowledgment of the Bible's importance. To this extent they seem to be a centripetal movement. Other characteristics of theirs propel them in a centrifugal direction. The most important factor in this regard is their supplementation of the Bible with the *Book of Mormon, Doctrine and Covenants,* and *The Pearl of Great Price.*[1] God is said in the first of these books to admit the incompleteness of earlier revelation in the Old and New Testament thus: 'Thou fool, that shall say: A Bible, we have got a Bible, and we need no more Bible. ... Wherefore, because that ye have a Bible, ye need not suppose that it contains all my words; neither need ye suppose that I have not caused more to be written.'[2] It is the post biblical 'revelations' that create the greatest difficulties in the way of an encounter, as in the case of Christian Science. But it is always possible, however unlikely at present, that later revelations from the presidents of the Mormons may encourage a return to the acceptance of the primacy of the original Bible.

In theory, Jehovah's Witnesses, as a biblically-based movement, ought to be moving towards the historic churches. In fact, it is centrifugal and as anti-ecclesiastical as any religious movement could be. It is an immensely courageous and a formidably cohesive movement. It is so cohesive and so autocratically controlled that it does not, at least for the present, seem open to encounter. This is partly because its members are predominantly still socially disinherited and have every reason for being suspicious of the well-to-do. It is partly that their cohesion consists in being united in the belief that all other religious groups are wholly in the wrong and they are wholly in the right. It is also partly due to the inflexible power of their leadership. Perhaps it is most of all due to their understanding of God (at least as it appears on the outside) which seems to be a combination of militancy to the many and mercy to the very few. One has sadly to conclude that any real encounter is almost impossible.

British-Israel is an ideology held by certain conservative Christians in the English-speaking part of the world, and not a separate religious organization complete with a separate creed, rites and ceremonies. It is only one significant example of a nationalistic and racialistic distortion which misrepresents the universalistic implications of Christ's gospel. Many other Christians in many denominations are also distorted by racial prejudices of a similar kind, though not articulated so thoroughly or disseminated so openly. These, whether British-Israel or the more vehement and cruel Klu Klux Klan, are indisputably the 'foes of our own household'. (These are vision-blocking splinters in the eyes of the historic churches which should prevent the churchly kettles from calling new movements black pots.)

Many factors might be the grounds of hope for a happy encounter between Christian Science and the ecumenical movement. These would include: the 'Christian' in the title, the requirement of regular public and private readings from the Bible, and a great renewal of interest in faith-healing on the part of many of the historic churches. Moreover, the Christian Scientists are a cheerful and helpful cross-section of the middle and upper-middle classes. Furthermore, one of their chaplains was linked with three others in death while saving lives on a torpedoed ship during World War II and is commemorated in the Four Chaplains Window of the chapel of Boston University. The real barrier is that the Bible is supplemented by a secondary source of revelation, *Science and Health*, which is the authoritative 'key' to unlock the scriptures. Moreover, that volume, however many its genuine spiritual insights are, is a compound of American Transcendentalism and Oriental immateriality which cannot be squared with the religion of the Incarnation. Change is not likely while the Board of Trustees are motivated by an inflexible archaism. Thus socially there is a centripetal movement, and ideologically there is a centrifugal movement. Any genuine encounter looks exceedingly improbable for the immediate future.

Scientology and Theosophy are, in the strictest sense, alternatives to Christianity, not 'deviations' from Christianity. The latter is an amalgam of religions. Scientology is a technique for mental improvement, not a religion of salvation. Neither, therefore, is likely to amalgamate with Christianity. The same is true of Spiritualism in general, though not of the specifically Christian Spiritualists.

It will be clear, then, that the likeliest immediate encounters will take place within those new spiritual movements which approximate to Protestantism in the primacy accorded to the Bible over tradition.

III

But what attitudes and actions on the part of individuals or groups within the historic churches are likely to encourage the centripetal movements?

It is abundantly clear that an essential preparation for the new encounter will be a *new attitude*. On our side of the divide there must be a new openness and a new humility. It can be helped by the recalling of some crucial facts and convictions.

We can begin by recognizing (as I have tried to do in earlier chapters) the great strengths of all these movements which have won them convinced adherents. It is clear that these values will be best expounded by those holding them rather than by the most sympathetic observer.

Then we might reflect that many of our so-called 'historic churches' were regarded by the 'more historic churches' as interlopers and schismatics when they originated. This is true of the Baptists and Congregationalists in the sixteenth century (as of the earlier Lutherans and Presbyterians of the same century) and of the Methodists of the eighteenth century. These denominations were originally even hostile to one another. Now the historic churches are seen to be the allies of the more historic churches, and it is desirable that we should anticipate the judgment of history in the case of the new movements.

A very sobering fact is that all Christendom is in fact in schism. It is true that most denominations are unhappy to remain as 'separated brethren', but separated they are. So are the members of the new movements that are Christian in intention. We are all members of the same convoy of Christians traversing the stormy waters of the present. Even if we interpret the Commander-in-Chief's signals with some differences, we none of us intend to flout his authority. Or, to be more precise, we debate about how faithfully some of the captains have relayed the orders.

We should also consider that the purpose of an encounter is to give freely of our convictions and of our doubts and to receive the same. We may pride ourselves on our church order as if it were part of the very gospel itself, but it may be the result of absolutizing the finite and confounding our preferences with the divine will for all men. We may rightly treasure our catholicity (in the sense of the wealth of guidance we inherit from many centuries and saints and their devotional, sacramental and ethical practice). We may be rightly grateful for the rich heritage of a Christian culture in music, art and architecture. But this inheritance is to be spent, given away, not hoarded, and our new friends have need of it as we did. Their ardour and vital experimentation in witness is what they have to give to us. It is only in encounter that we shall learn what gifts have to be exchanged and what confessions and reparations must be made.

Supremely, we and they need together to learn the art of speaking and acting the truth in love. This cannot be done without deep and continuing mutual involvement on the part of the older and the newer denominations. If the danger in the past has been speaking the truth dogmatically (as if it were our truth and not God's), the danger of the present could be that we speak not lovingly but sentimentally and achieve only a relationship of cordial ambiguity. Thus we would fall a prey to doctrinal relativism. (I do not forget that Chesterton remarked that the effect of studying comparative religions was to make one only comparatively religious!)

We are more likely to attain that attitude of speaking and acting the truth in love if we recollect that it was as the compassionate Servant of God that Jesus won his way into the hearts of men, and that he forbade his disciples to lord it over others, but told them to serve them.

Above all, we should constantly remember that Christ has sheep 'not of this fold' who hear his voice, and that *he* knows his own. We believe that he will ultimately bring them into one fold, and it is not our job to erect barbed wire fences of suspicion and hostility, but to demolish them. If we – on the side of the historic Christian churches – are ever inclined to think God's other charges are black sheep or worse, sheep in wolves' clothing – the terrible darkening of the inner eye that Pharisaism produces – then we must look to the wolf within us. We all need the grace which God in Christ bestows undeservingly on each. This is the best spirit in which to work for *rapprochement.*

But holy attitudes must be expressed in holy actions. And perhaps the holiest are those which are done without hope of earthly fruit. If that be so, we must not consider the most improbable encounter fruitless. But it is good Christian strategy also to concentrate on the most probable objectives. These actions in which we engage as individuals or as members of groups will demand an overcoming of suspicion by an honest and cordial meeting of minds and hearts. Each reader will have his or her own ideas how to improve the contacts which every day or every week brings for the work of reconciliation. It would be impertinent for me to try to say, if I could, how keen individuals will find the way.

But, apart from the important individual meetings for dialogue, there must be opportunities for a more official but no less friendly encounter. Young people's groups in local churches could arrange to meet their opposite numbers in the new movements. Local churches or delegations from them could arrange for exchanges of preaching and worship. Local clergy and ministers could invite local leaders of the new movements to join their fraternal if the good feeling were to be reciprocated. And there is the great need for such action at denominational levels.

For long the Anglican and Lutheran communions have acted as 'bridge-churches' because of their strategic position straddling

Index

Sabbath, the, 22-33
Salt Lake City, Utah, 2, 5, 47f., 51
Santayana, George, 22
Scientology, 104-110, 115, 119, 127
Seventh-Day Adventism, 2, 5f., 25-33, 77, 114f., 120, 123, 125
Smith, Joseph, 6, 48f., 54, 56f., 119, 130
Socialism, 65, 87
Sociological factors, 1-14, 122f.
Söderblom, Bishop Nathan, 6
South Africa, Republic of, 2, 4, 5, 10, 89
Spiritualism, 2, 5, 67-75, 114-116, 118f., 127
Stroup, H. H., 65, 66
Studd, Commander, 77, 79
Sundkler, Bishop Bengt, 10, 13

Tappert, Theodore, 88
Temple, Archbishop William, 1, 6
Theosophy, 94, 95-103, 115, 117f., 127
Thomas, Robert, 105

Thornton-Duesbery, J. P., 86, 92, 94
Tithing, 25, 48

Union Theological Seminary, N.Y.C., 123

Van Baalen, J. K., 14, 66
Verbal infallibility (of the Bible), 10, 77, 113, 125

Watchtower Organization, the, *see* Jehovah's Witnesses
Wesley, John, 12
White, Ellen, 27-33
Wilbur, Sybil, 45
Williams, Donald, 17
Women's roles in religion, 27, 37f., 104, 117

Yale University, 123
Young, Brigham, 51

Zen Buddhism, 24